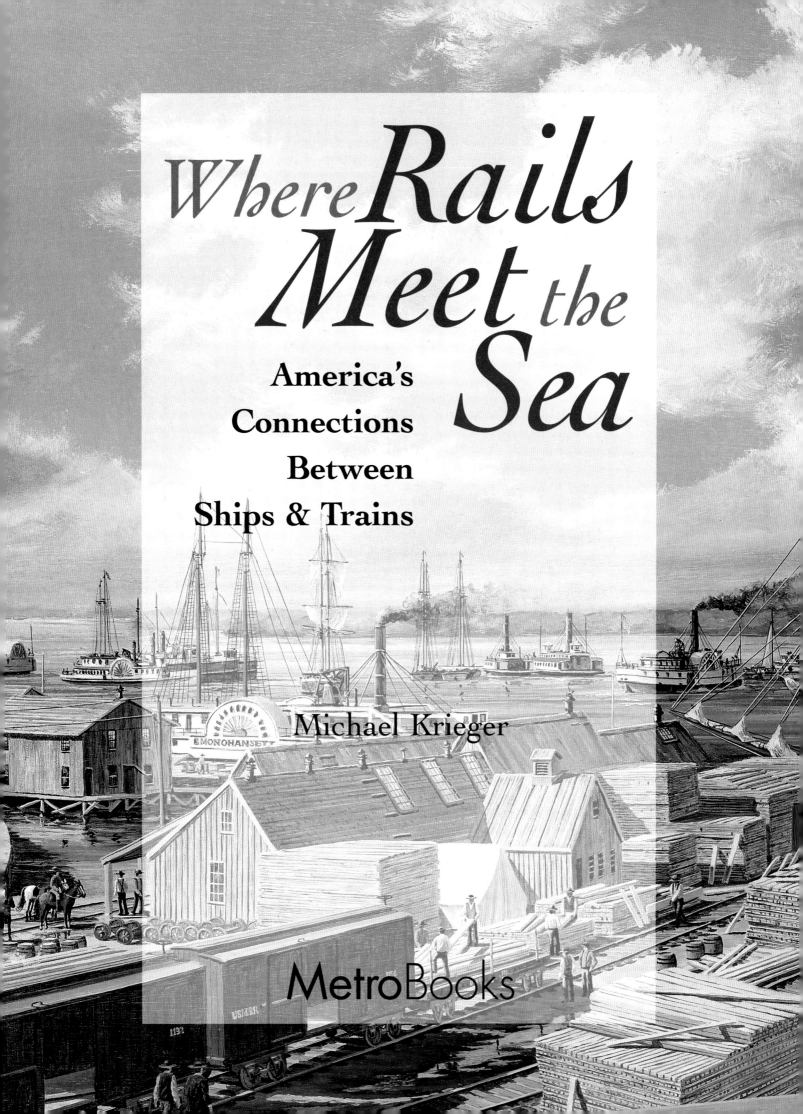

Where *Rails* Meet *the* Sea

America's Connections Between Ships & Trains

Michael Krieger

MetroBooks

MetroBooks

An Imprint of Friedman/Fairfax Publishers

Text copyright © 1998 Michael Krieger

Copyright © 1998 by
Michael Friedman Publishing Group, Inc.

ISBN 1-56799-597-7

Library of Congress Cataloging-in-Publication
Data available upon request.

Editor: Nathaniel Marunas
Art Director: Kevin Ullrich
Designer: Lori Thorn
Photography Editors: Michael Krieger
    and Sarah Storey
Production Manager: Susan Kowal

Color separations by
Colourscan Overseas Co Pte Ltd
Printed in Italy by Poligrafiche Bolis S.p.A.

10   9   8   7   6   5   4   3   2   1
For bulk purchases and special sales,
please contact:
Friedman/Fairfax Publishers
Attention: Sales Department
15 West 26th Street
New York, NY 10010
(212) 685-6610 fax: (212) 685-1307

Visit our website: http://www.metrobooks.com

Front jacket: See page 122.

Front endpaper: See page 146.

Pages 2–3: In June 1864 General Grant, in his campaign to capture Richmond, the capital and heart of
the Confederacy, ordered that City Point, Virginia, be
established at the junction of the James and
Appomattox rivers as the Union's supply base.
Construction Corps battalions worked feverishly to
rebuild the wharves, warehouses, tracks, and terminal facilities of the Old City Point Railroad that had
been destroyed in previous fighting. Within a month,
rail service was established eight miles (12.8km)
west. Track and facilities continued to grow, and by
early 1865, the time depicted in this William
McGrath painting, City Point had been developed
into a sizable complex. Other Southern railroads—the
South Side, the Petersburg, and the Norfolk &
Petersburg—were also used.

Page 7: This inaugural brochure for the Florida East
Coast Railroad's Key West Extension commemorates
the daunting technical achievement completed in
1912. Ten thousand people celebrated America's
longest rail line built over open water, 126 miles
(201.6km) from the southern tip of Florida to the
island of Key West. Shown is Long Key Viaduct, built
over two miles (3.2km) of open water.

Page 8: In 1849 the Baltimore and Ohio opened a new
marine terminal in Baltimore at Locust Point. In
addition to coal, Locust Point handled grain and general merchandise, and was an important port for
immigrant vessels. This painting by Herbert Still
shows a B&O passenger train, circa 1872, greeting
immigrants from a French vessel (left) and possibly
a Canadian one (right), which is flying the Red
Duster, Britain's maritime (merchant) flag.

Back endpaper: See page 142.

Back jacket: See page 125.

ACKNOWLEDGMENTS

While a great many people helped to ready this little vessel for sea, as captain I claim responsibility for any and all errors. Then, starting with those closest to home, I would like to thank my wife, Susan, for her patience and support throughout this project; my assistant, Sue Ann Fazio, for her diligent typing and checking of the millions of details; and editor Carol Bee, who, as always, is my guru of grammar and punctuation.

From every coast, people contributed their knowledge and, in some cases, their personal photo collections. Thank you, Paul Haas of the State Historical Society of Wisconsin; William Kooiman of the San Francisco Maritime Museum; John Appleyard; Donald Davis; John Grecol; William Worden; Pat Labadie, U.S. Army Corps of Engineers, Duluth Interpretive Center; Gordon Bugbee; Stan Melman of the Hawaiian Maritime Center; Jenny Watts of the Huntington Museum; Susan Carter and Melinda Chavetz of the Plant Museum; Nancy Russell and Bart Nadeau, formerly of Southern Pacific Railroad; George Werner; Tom Moungovan; Claudia Jew of the Mariners' Museum; Tom Leary; Steve Hauff; and Leon Callaway.

A few experts and collectors provided very special help. I wish to extend extra appreciation to Connie Hoffman, Ralph Roberts, Louis Saillard, John Signor, George Hilton, George Johnson, and Steve Cryan.

DEDICATION

Although many people from around the country contributed to this book, two people, both experts on eastern rail/marine history, gave more than I could have expected from anyone and especially improved this work. It is with the most heartfelt gratitude that I dedicate *Where Rails Meet the Sea* to Tom Flagg and to John Teichmoeller.

CONTENTS

OFFICIAL PROGRAM AND SOUVENIR

KEY WEST EXTENSION

OF THE

FLORIDA·EAST·COAST·RAILWAY

"THE OVER-SEA RAILROAD"

Price 25¢

Locust Point – Marine Terminus
in the Early Eighties

PREFACE

The second half of the nineteenth century brought a transportation explosion in America and Europe, much of it produced by the steam engine. Though the steam engine had been widely used prior to 1850, it was a sputtering, trouble-prone fuel-eater capable of propelling a railway engine or small vessel only short distances. Not until the first compound engines became available in the 1850s could ships really go to sea. Likewise, not until bigger fireboxes and larger and more numerous driving wheels were introduced could railway engines make any speed or travel beyond the next village.

The ships and the trains met, of course, at ports that had previously been the domain of companies owning sailing ships or horse-drawn wagons. Thus, during the second half of the nineteenth century a new influence came to power in many of our coastal cities. The shrewd businessmen who led the nation's burgeoning railroads understood only too well that to control the flow of goods and people through America's ports was to dominate transport throughout large sections of the country. At first, city fathers were wildly enthusiastic about the coming of a railroad. Later, when they saw how a railroad that controlled the port could strangle their city, they tried to regain control—to no avail, in some cases.

Frequently, the railroads fought bitterly among themselves to gain access to the port cities and to prevent their rivals from sharing the wealth. Certain railroads, realizing that they could extend their influence to other parts of the country (and, indeed, to other parts of the world) that they couldn't reach on their own tracks, created fleets of ships to carry their freight and passengers to more distant markets. Thus, America's original transportation conglomerates were born.

While this book aims to provide a general history of the railroads' maritime presence and their effect on the growth of America's ports, there simply is not space enough to cover the development of the nation's river ports, much less the ports of Canada or Mexico. Indeed, hundreds of pages more could be written on just the primary focus of this book.

❧ INTRODUCTION ☙
THE EARLY DAYS

Part of Buffalo's inner harbor was the City Ship Canal, which extended five miles (8km) from the Buffalo River mouth. Excavation was completed in 1880, and by 1888, the date of this photograph, it was lined with docks, grain elevators, and warehouses. Within the next twenty years steel mills and then oil refineries would be added. In the foreground is the South Michigan Street Bridge. On the far bank are tracks of the Buffalo Creek Railroad, a terminal belt-line owned jointly by the Lehigh Valley and Erie railroads. On the side of the Frontier, the first elevator at left, is a "marine leg," which extends into a ship's hold and has buckets affixed to a conveyor. This steam-powered apparatus revolutionized vessel grain loading and discharging.

Settlements in early America lay scattered like sand along narrow strips of coastal land. The largest towns usually developed around a good port, and the fastest-growing also bordered navigable rivers that facilitated the movement of goods and people inland. Not until the advent of the steamboat in the 1820s, however, could rivers be used easily. Nor could roads then provide reliable transport. They were dusty, rutted axle-breakers in summer and impassable bogs much of the rest of the year. As the country grew, towns and then small cities sprang up farther and farther from the coasts.

Still, no dependable means existed to connect them to the port cities.

Some paved toll roads could be seen as early as 1800, and by 1812 more than five thousand miles (8,000km) of them meandered, usually inland. But turnpikes were expensive to build, and transporting people, produce, and merchandise required something faster than horse and wagon. As a result, canals, which could connect navigable rivers to each other or to lakes, gained great favor. By 1800 a twenty-two-mile (35.2km) canal connected the Cooper and Santee rivers in South Carolina. Other, shorter canals also existed, and

A girl tends her family's two mules pulling their canal boat along the Delaware and Hudson Canal. The D&H Canal Company was formed in 1825 to build a 108-mile (172.8km) waterway from Honesdale, Pennsylvania, to Eddyville, New York, and by connecting with the Hudson River, to bring coal to New York City. The eastern canals were the first attempt at creating a new transportation system in the United States.

A South Carolina Railroad three-dollar note dating from the 1830s. The South Carolina and many other railroads were permitted by state governments to help raise money by starting banks and by issuing their own currency. Much of this currency was designed and printed in Britain or Europe and often illustrated by artists who knew little about what they were representing. The locomotive pictured is not the Best Friend of Charleston, but likely some artist's wild interpretation of what he thought it might look like.

more were planned. By the 1820s avid canal builders were digging nearly everywhere they could find fairly flat land and enough water to fill their ditches. The Delaware and Hudson, the Morris, the Union, the Chesapeake and Ohio, and the Lehigh were well under way. However, it was the opening of the first major canal in the United States, the Erie in 1825, that gave the canal builders promise of great rewards to come.

The Erie Canal, stretching 363 miles (580.8km) from the Hudson River near Albany all the way to Lake Erie at Buffalo, proved an instant success. Not only could it move western New York farm goods to the coast, but it established the first real connection to the growing Midwest. For the first time New York

City businesses could trade readily with Cleveland, Detroit, or Toledo as travel was shortened to weeks instead of months. Only sixteen years later the trip, via steamboat and railroad, would be further reduced—to less than three days. In the meantime, canals were the preferred mode of transport, though they turned out to be surprisingly expensive to maintain, and in the winter the northern ones froze solid. Also, they could only be built in the few places with suitable topography. Soon people began to look toward the small, chugging iron horse and its waterborne counterpart, the steamboat, to fulfill America's transportation destiny.

The first commercial railroad train in the United States bumped and rattled behind the Baltimore

and Ohio's *Tom Thumb* in 1838 between Baltimore and Ellicott's Mills, Maryland. Following close behind were the South Carolina Canal and Railroad's *Best Friend of Charleston* and the Mohawk and Hudson's De Witt Clinton, which ran on a route parallel to the Erie Canal from Albany to Schenectady. The *John Bull* pulled the first passenger train between New York City and Philadelphia in 1831 for the Camden and Amboy Railroad. It also inaugurated the first rail/steamboat combination, utilizing passenger ferries over the Delaware River to Philadelphia and from Amboy across lower New York Bay to Manhattan.

In the 1830s small railroads sprouted like wildflowers throughout the East and South. By 1835 more than one thousand miles (1,600km) of railroad lines provided service. Nonetheless, they were primitive, rickety, bone-jarring, smoke-filled, spark-shooting, breakdown-prone nuisances at first—hardly the sophisticated transporters they would soon become. Steamboat lines multiplied as well, first in the sheltered waters of rivers and harbors, then on the lakes and the sea. Together, the steamships and trains would create America's first transportation revolution.

Seen here, the race between the Baltimore & Ohio Railroad's *Tom Thumb* and a horse, said to have taken place August 28, 1830, was one of a number of early "test races" to see which was faster—animal or machine. In this case the horse got the jump, but the *Tom Thumb* caught up and appeared to be winning when a band slipped off a pulley. Before the piece could be refit, the gallant horse claimed victory. From a painting by H.D. Stitt.

CHAPTER ONE
THE EAST

In 1944 freight arriving by barge or lighter from around New York Harbor is sorted and loaded into outbound freight cars in CRRNJ's Jersey City waterfront terminal. A checker at the boxcar door tallies barrels being loaded.

New England

On a freezing February night in 1845, John Poor, a young lawyer, set out during a blizzard on a grueling 250-mile (400km) sleigh ride from Portland, Maine, to Montreal. His ride would change the course of New England's transportation history. The prize he sought for Portland was to be chosen as the port for Montreal, Canada, already a large community on the St. Lawrence River that was icebound all winter. Montreal's Board of Trade had decided to build a railroad to connect their city with an all-year, ice-free New England port. Emissaries from Boston had recently convinced the trade board members that their thriving city should be the choice.

Two lumber schooners at Brown's Wharf, Portland, Maine, in 1924. This is an interesting scene for modelers. Note how the tracks of Maine Central's subsidiary, Portland Terminal Company, run down the middle of the wharf rather than along the sides, where direct car-to-vessel loading and discharging could take place. This is typical of premechanized lumber loading, when each stick of lumber was carried to or from the vessels. Also, this allowed the on-site office to sell lumber locally for dray removal as well as to ship it by rail. Schooners probably brought the timber from "Down East" (Maine's northeastern coastal areas) or from Canada's maritime provinces. Across Casco Bay South, Portland appears in the distance.

John Poor heard on February 5 that the Boston selection would formally be voted on at a Montreal meeting on February 10. Immediately, he set out with a friend for Montreal through snow so deep that their horse often pulled them over stone walls and woodpiles rather than the road. Poor hired new teams and guides as they went. Stopping at inns and farmhouses only long enough to warm themselves, they arrived in Montreal five days later, exhausted, just a few hours before the meeting.

That evening the eloquent young lawyer not only convinced the board that Portland was better situated than Boston, being closer both to Montreal and to European ports, but told them that Portland already had a railroad charter and would pay for the entire line to the Canadian border. Portland triumphed, and in 1853 the new railroad, called the Atlantic and St. Lawrence, was completed. That same year a well-financed new Canadian line, the Grand Trunk Line of Canada, took a 999-year lease on the Atlantic and St. Lawrence. Large amounts of money were spent for new terminal facilities in Portland, and a year-round line of steamers began service to Liverpool, England.

By 1850 Portland was connected to Boston and points south by no fewer than three competing roads: the Boston and Maine, the Eastern, and the Portland, Saco & Portsmouth. The three railroads, notwithstanding their rivalry, joined to build a fine side-wheel steamer, the *Daniel Webster*, to operate between Portland and Bangor in northern Maine. Portland was also diverting Boston exports. Shippers were told that because Portland was closer to northern European ports, they could save time shipping through Maine. Boston shipping companies were, of course, furious and tried to debunk the claims, saying that Portland's location, only one hundred miles (160km) north of Boston, meant little in cross-Atlantic voyage times. Boston, moreover, had even greater problems with its rivals to the south.

This sailing notice for the new steamer *Eastern Queen* was dated 1857. She and the *Star of the East* were to meet trains of the Penobscot & Kennebec and the Androscoggin railroads, both running east and connecting Portland, Lewiston, Waterville, and Bangor. These railroads were consolidated in 1862 to form the Maine Central, which subsequently leased the Portland & Kennebec, providing important trackage south to Portland. Portland and Boston had rail connections by the mid-1860s. Both the Boston & Maine and the Eastern railroads served the two cities, and each had its own steamship subsidiary bringing passengers from Rockland and points north.

The Berkshire Hills run north and south along the western boundaries of Massachusetts and Connecticut. Today they appear just as low hills, certainly no obstacle to building a canal or a railroad line. But in 1830 they were a formidable barrier, isolating Boston from the rich agricultural lands to the west. Not only was Boston cut off from the west, it was nearly as isolated from prospering New York and other areas to the south; reaching New York required a two-day steamer journey or an even longer overland haul on the poorly maintained post road. Boston merchants and shipowners watched enviously as the Erie Canal and New York's budding railroads siphoned western trade that Bostonians felt should be theirs. Boston's struggles to maintain her share of the transportation pie would span one hundred and fifty years.

By 1846, however, great improvements had been made in connecting New England and New York. Two Massachusetts railroads, the Old Colony and the Fall River, were meeting New York–bound steamers at Plymouth and Fall River. Soon the two railroads decided to cooperate, and in May 1847 the first Boat Train, the vessel *Bay State*, met the Old Colony Railroad passenger special from Boston and departed Fall River for New York City. The famous Boat Train ran for ninety years, making it America's longest continuous railroad passenger service.

Although the Fall River Line of steamboats—which was always connected with the Old Colony Railroad or its successor, the New York, New Haven, and Hartford—was the most famous railroad/steamer service, it was only one of a number of competitors vying for New York–New England supremacy. The Boston and Providence, the Providence and Worcester, and the New York, Providence, and Boston railroads all had established steamer connections to New York, but by the turn of the century most of these short lines would be gobbled up by larger roads intent on capturing this most lucrative of markets. The railroad that would dominate both New England's rail and

The Boston & Maine Railroad depot in Salem, Massachusetts, as seen around 1890, was located at the corner of Washington and Norman streets, just a short distance from the harbor. It was built in 1847 and originally served the Eastern Railroad before it was taken over by the B&M. The building was demolished in 1954.

shipping, however, was not the New York Central, the Pennsylvania, or the Erie, but the New York, New Haven, and Hartford—known as the New Haven.

Though nearly all the larger railroads in the Northeast operated steamships to extend their markets beyond the limits of their rail systems, the New Haven was the Goliath. By 1899 it had taken control of the Fall River Line of steamers, having leased the Old Colony Railroad (which itself had already absorbed the Fall River Railroad in order to dominate transportation in southern Connecticut). The New Haven had also acquired a majority interest in four more steamship lines (the

Providence, the Norwich, the Stonington, and the New Bedford) and would soon control the New Haven and the Bridgeport steamship companies as well.

Charles Mellen—a railroad tycoon, banker, and protégé of J.P. Morgan—had decided to make himself king of New England transportation by acquiring all the region's major railroads and steamship companies. With almost unlimited funds he quickly put together his empire. By 1903 he controlled and was president of the New Haven Railroad. By 1907 he had acquired the Boston and Maine Railroad, the Maine Central, and jointly with the New York Central, the Rutland Railroad. He also gained control of seven more steamship companies, and despite continual antitrust litigation and investigations by the Interstate Commerce Commission (ICC), Mellen succeeded in gaining a near monopoly on rail and shipping in southern New England.

Right and below: Two views of Maine Central's steamer, the *Ferdinando Gorges*. The rail-car ferry was built in 1909 by Bath Iron Works. She was 240 feet (73m) long, weighed 1,361 gross tons (1,382.8t), and could carry eight passenger cars on her three tracks. She ferried trains across the Kennebec River at Bath along with an older sister, the *Hercules*. Eventually, in 1927, she was replaced by a bridge. The *Gorges* was named for the Portuguese explorer who reputedly discovered Maine.

MAINE CENTRAL
RAILROAD COMPANY

Right: Maine Central's little steamer *Sebanoa*, weighing eighty-nine tons (90.4t) and ninety-one feet (27.7m) long, was built in 1880 in Bath, Maine. Maine Central bought her in 1884 and used her from Bath to Booth Bay and then to Bar Harbor from the railhead at Mt. Desert Ferry, and finally between Dark Harbor, Islesboro, and Rockland. Maine Central and its subsidiary, the Portland, Mt. Desert & Machias Steamboat Co., had a sizable fleet of steamers serving most of the Maine coast and connecting with trains at Portland, Rockland, Mount Desert Ferry, and Calais. Its largest steamers were the *City of Richmond* (875 tons [889t], 227 feet [69m], built in 1865), which ran between Portland, Bar Harbor, and Machiasport, and the *Frank Jones* (1,634 tons [1,660t], 263 feet [80m], built in 1892), which ran from Boston to Mt. Desert via Portland. Maine Central's boat trains operated until 1960, totaling nearly ninety years of continuous service.

Opposite: The Maine Central had routing throughout its home state as well as into northern Vermont and New Hampshire. In 1869 it merged into its chief competitor, the Eastern Railroad, and in 1883 the Boston & Maine leased the Eastern and with it took control of the Maine Central. This arrangement lasted until 1914. The B&M and Maine Central continued to work together, even sharing corporate officers, until 1952. In the early 1980s both railroads were purchased by the Mellen family. In this illustration, a telegraph operator hands the engineer of a Maine Central F-3 diesel his train orders on the end of an order stick.

Above: An artist's conception of the Fall River Terminal, the apex of boat-train connections between Boston and New York. Inaugurated on May 18, 1847, the "boat train" served the two cities for ninety years, certainly an American record and probably a world record. An Old Colony Railroad train waits at the station for passengers arriving by steamboat from New York. The steamship depictions, while not totally accurate, probably represent the *Bay State* (white hull), 315 feet (95.8m) and fifteen hundred tons (1,524t), or her sister, the *Massachusetts*, both owned by the Bay State Steamboat Company, later known as the Fall River Line. The black-hulled vessel generally resembles any one of three freighters the line owned.

From 1847 to 1917 the fastest way to reach New York City from Boston was by a boat train. The most popular of them all and the one that received the greatest accolades for both luxury and convenience was "The Boat Train," operated by the Fall River Line.

If you were a Boat Train passenger bound for New York City in the 1890s, you departed Boston's South Station early in the evening, boarding, perhaps, the new steel-hulled steamer *Puritan* at Fall River an hour and a half later. You then enjoyed a delightful evening at sea, for the public rooms and accommodations on the *Puritan* and her sisters were plush, with beautiful joinery, expensive carpets, grand staircases, and gorgeous staterooms. You would also dine well. Many critics favorably compared Boat Train food and service to those in New York's finer restaurants. Then, rested and refreshed, you arrived early the next morning in downtown Manhattan.

Despite Mellen's tactics of buying out the competition or forcing it out of business, his steamship companies always had at least a few rivals. Enterprise Transportation began in 1905 and the Joy Line in 1906. Each had only a small num-

Part of Boston's Atlantic Avenue waterfront in 1906. The Metropolitan Steamship Line, on India Wharf, offered an all-water route to Manhattan. The steamer *H.M. Whitney*, named after the company's owner, appears to be transferring cargo to or from boxcars on a carfloat lying alongside. The loaded carfloats were transferred to New Haven's floatbridge, just north of their Pier 4 in South Boston, for dispatch to outbound trains. The coastal steamer *Prince George* makes her way out of the harbor.

Right: The Fall River Line's *Puritan*, built in 1889, was a remarkable vessel for her time. She was the first ship in Long Island Sound service to exceed 400' (403') and to have a steel hull, and she had the largest compound-walking-beam engine then constructed. Her record for the 176-mile voyage from New York to Fall River was eight hours and twenty-four minutes, an average of over 20 miles an hour. Ex-President Grover Cleveland was a passenger on the palatial vessel, which served until 1908. She was then relegated to standby duty until 1915, when she was scrapped.

Above: Bags of cotton or wool in a sling slide up a loading ramp before being lowered into a ship's hold. This procedure reduced the risk of a valuable bag slipping out of the sling and being damaged. New England was still America's textile capital and the nation's major exporter of cloth. The scene is likely adjacent to the New Haven's South Boston terminal and its grain elevator, the latter being demolished prior to 1935.

ber of vessels operating from New England ports to New York. But it was the Boston Line, owned by Hudson River steamship magnate C.W. Morse, that was to give Charles Mellen conniption fits and provide his only serious competition. When Mellen refused Morse's offer of $20 million to buy all of the New Haven's steamship interests, Morse built two of the largest, fastest, and most handsome liners to sail Long Island Sound. Traveling at speeds of up to 23 knots, the *Harvard* and the *Yale* were each 400-foot (121.6m) vessels that sailed directly from Boston to New York City. They were extremely popular even though they plied a rough-weather route around Cape Cod. In 1911 they forced Mellen's Boston Merchants Line to develop its own "outside fleet," the *Massachusetts* and the *Bunker Hill*.

Top right: Downtown Boston in 1925, seen with, in the foreground, team tracks of the South Boston Freight Terminal. Out of sight are the terminal's piers, freight houses, and locomotive roundhouse. For some years, Union Freight had tracks across Fort Point Channel on the Northern Avenue swing bridge. On the right are two of the Nantasket Line's vessels. Behind them, the tall building is the Custom House Tower, built in 1915 and for many years the tallest building in Boston.

Bottom right: In 1925 Boston's North End waterfront included (from right to left) Central Wharf, Long Wharf, and, diagonally, Commercial Wharf. In front of the wharves are two rail lines. The elevated is the Boston Elevated Railway, one of the city's private transit systems, which had passenger lines running along the harbor and ending at the terminal for the East Boston ferry. The street-level line was the Union Freight Railroad, a belt line that moved freight cars between the Boston & Maine's North Boston yards along Atlantic Avenue and the New Haven's South Boston Freight Terminal. Across the harbor on the right are the piers of the Boston & Albany's East Boston Freight Terminal and behind them a New York Central System grain elevator.

Opposite: Boston's South Station in 1930; it opened in 1899, and for some years was considered the largest and busiest railroad station in the United States. It was the northern terminus for both the New York, New Haven, & Hartford, with its tracks on the right, and the Boston & Albany, with its tracks on the left. South Station was also a boat-train terminal with connections to many of the New Haven's steamship subsidiaries. The bridges on the right, from front to back, are the Summer Street, the Congress Street, and the Northern Avenue.

By 1930 the New Haven had consolidated all its steamship companies into the New England Steamship Lines, which operated thirteen passenger vessels, some with auto capacity, to New York City and between the larger New England ports. However, in spite of their efforts to build more modern and faster vessels, New England Steam and the other steamship operators were on their way out. In 1917 the Pennsylvania Railroad (PRR) and the New Haven had opened a railroad bridge over the Hell's Gate Narrows and initiated direct trains between Boston and New York City. All-rail commuting to New York proved to be both faster and cheaper than going by vessel. This, together with the development of a modern highway system, put one steamship company after another into bankruptcy. In 1937 both the New Haven Railroad and its Fall River Line, the last passenger steamship operator on the Sound, went bankrupt. Thus ended ninety years of continual service by the famous Boat Train.

In spite of, or maybe because of, improved transportation connections between New England and New York, Boston and other northeastern ports continued to lose ground in shipping both imports and exports. Boston's export business declined severely, from 1,300,000 tons (1,320,800t) shipped in 1905 to only 321,400 tons (326,542.4t) shipped in 1938. Indeed, by 1949 over 65 percent (valuation) of New England's manufactured goods intended for export were shipped through New York harbor and only 14 percent through Boston harbor. Unfavorable rail freight rates, in comparison with such competing ports as Philadelphia and Baltimore, accounted for some loss of cargoes. New York gave shippers free lighterage, moving their cargoes across the harbor at no charge. This was expensive for those railroads whose fleets of tugs, barges, and carfloats were used, but offset the natural advantage of such ports as Boston, where all the docks were serviced directly by railroad tracks. Thus, ships berthed on the island of Manhattan could be loaded or unloaded at no extra cost to the cargoes' owners. New York railroads often offered other special inducements to shippers, too, such as below-cost warehousing, drayage, and handling charges. As a result, increasing numbers of steamship companies began to offer more frequent sailings to all parts of the world from New York while fewer and fewer such sailings were leaving from competing ports such as Boston.

Why didn't New England's railroads provide offsetting rebates to Boston's shippers? For one simple reason: by the 1920s all three principal railroads serving New England were controlled by larger trunk lines whose interests were best served by the status quo. The Pennsylvania Railroad owned a controlling interest in the New York, New Haven, and Hartford, which in turn controlled the Boston and Maine. New York Central had a long-term lease on the Boston and Albany Railroad, which allowed it to set policy for the smaller road. So the Port of New York flourished and the Port of Boston continued to suffer.

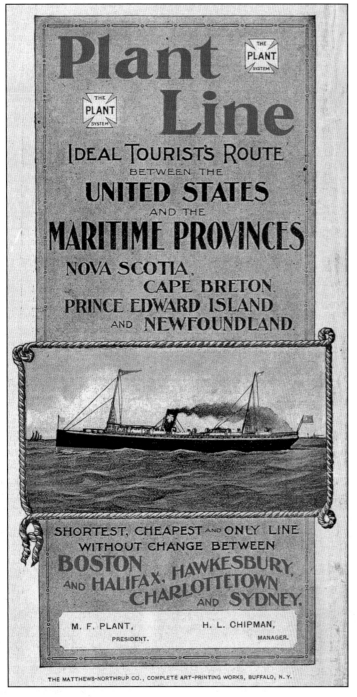

A Plant System brochure, circa 1895, advertising its summer excursion route between Boston and the Canadian maritime provinces. During winter months the Plant System vessels would service the Gulf states and the Caribbean, catering largely to vacationers. Then in summer two vessels would transfer to Boston for twice-weekly Canadian sailings. The vessel pictured is *La Grande Duchesse*, 380 feet (115.5m) long and weighing 3,056 tons (3,104.9t).

Central Atlantic

wo other port cities battled for transportation parity with New York. In the years immediately following the Civil War the region's three major ports were each supported by a "flag carrier": New York, of course, by the New York Central; Baltimore by the Baltimore and Ohio; and Philadelphia by the Pennsylvania Railroad, newly chartered in 1846, but expanding rapidly to the west, where coal was already king. Soon, however, the three railroads' western expansion, particularly to the Great Lakes, together with competition from other trunk carriers—such as the Erie, the Lackawanna, and the Chesapeake and Ohio—forced the major lines to abandon parochial subservience to their base cities in favor of a more independent, regionalist approach.

Officials of the Pennsylvania and B&O railroads had tried to prevent competitors (each other and the New York Central) from acquiring rights into and through their respective key cities. When that tactic failed, both railroads realized that they must establish a strong New York presence or suffer. The reason was

Part of Baltimore Harbor, circa 1927, including the Canton Company's marine terminals in the foreground. The Canton Company, which would soon be controlled by the Pennsylvania Railroad, developed not only the terminal and attendant industrial park, but also the Canton Railroad, its own switching line. The second of the long, slender piers is the ore pier, at which a ship is unloading. Next to the ore pier is a floatbridge for docking railroad carfloats, a fertilizer facility, and then general and bulk-cargo piers served by the Pennsylvania Railroad. Across the water, on the upper left, in Locust Point, is Fort McHenry. Also visible are a large B&O grain elevator and, in the distance, Baltimore's inner harbor.

clear: already more ships were calling at New York than at Baltimore and Philadelphia combined. Vessel owners and shippers were able to shave days off their schedules by not negotiating Chesapeake Bay or the Delaware River and *then* having to sail farther north on their course to Liverpool or the other northern European ports. Already the die had been cast; both the steamship and the railroad industries were focused on New York.

On the night of March 11, 1868, there was no moon and a deep veil of fog shrouded New York harbor. The Hudson River, separating Manhattan and New Jersey, was especially dangerous. At any moment one of the many ferries, tugboats, barges, or steamships might suddenly loom out of the mist. On this night the Hudson was especially no place for a small boat, and yet in the middle of the river a rowboat with a single heaving oarsman and two passengers was thrashing through the water. Originally headed for the Jersey shore, it now was lost in the fog, yawing this

Above: A 1939 advertising piece for the Old Bay Line, which from 1894 was controlled by J.P. Morgan's Southern Railway; it eventually became a part of Seaboard Air Line Railway. The company's main route was between Baltimore and Norfolk. The boat pictured is the famous *President Warfield*. Built in 1928 for use only in Chesapeake Bay service, she and her sisters (the *State of Virginia* and the *State of Maryland*) were taken over by the military as troop transports in World War II and sailed in convoy for England in 1942. The convoy was attacked by a German submarine, and the *Warfield* was nearly hit by a torpedo. After the war, in 1947, she was purchased by Zionists in Germany to carry Jewish refugees to Palestine (what would become Israel). The four-hundred-passenger vessel, now renamed the *Exodus* and loaded with 4,554 refugees, was intercepted by a British naval blockade off the coast of Egypt. The refugees were returned to Germany and the *Exodus* was sunk in Haifa Harbor. Her first owner, the Old Bay Line, just prior to going out of business in 1962, was the oldest steamboat line in the United States.

Left: By 1910, when this photograph was taken, the Baltimore & Ohio Railroad had expanded its Locust Point, Baltimore, terminal. An immigrant-shipping joint venture with North German Lloyd begun in 1867 had expired in 1889, but the influx of immigrants continued and was a major passenger business for the B&O and nearly all the other trunk lines. The modern cargo liner pictured is built to carry a large number of passengers, and probably hers have just disembarked and are on the departing train. The wooden covered barges were used to transfer freight to vessels at anchor or moored to other piers.

Right: The side-wheel transfer steamer *Canton*, and then after her, the *John W. Garrett*, carried rail cars across Baltimore Harbor for the Baltimore & Ohio. The Canton had a two/three track configuration allowing loading and stability in either arrangement. The 324-foot (98.5m) vessel, built by Harlan and Hollingsworth in 1879, was cut down to a barge in 1886 and sent to New York Harbor. She ended her days back on the Chesapeake Bay as a Cape Charles, Norfolk rail car barge for the New York, Philadelphia & Norfolk Railroad.

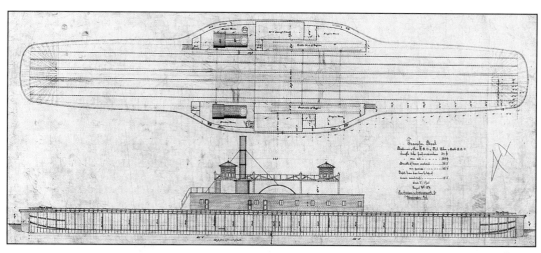

Opposite and above: An important source of traffic for the Baltimore and Ohio and the Pennsylvania Railroad at Baltimore was the movement of bananas. United Fruit ships are tied up at Pier 1, Pratt Street, where Harborplace is now. Downtown Baltimore can be seen in the background. In the view, above, the 1893 B&O tug *Baltimore* moves an old wooden two-track carfloat with refrigerator cars. The reefers would be brought alongside ships so that longshoremen could transfer the bananas. To keep the reefers from rolling off the carfloat, brake wheels would be set and timbers jammed in place outside the outer wheels. Toggle pockets on the ends of the floats hold one end of steel toggle bars when the floats are docked (the other end is locked in slots on the dock) to help maintain alignment.

A 1926 Norfolk & Western Railway brochure promotes railway-steamer excursions. With rail routes extending to New York, Chicago, Detroit, and Cleveland, the railroad tried to entice southern passengers to spend their summer vacations on the Great Lakes, at Niagara Falls, on lakes George and Champlain, along the Hudson River, and in Boston and Maine—all destinations the Norfolk & Western's tracks didn't reach—via rail-steamboat "package tours." Rail-steamboat excursions were sold by many railroads around the country and were the forerunners of today's package tours.

way and that as the frightened and exasperated passengers ordered the rower according to their whim. Then, from nowhere, a ferry bore down on them. Terrified, all three men screamed at the top of their lungs. The helmsman saw or heard them, and at the last moment the ferry veered away. It just missed killing two of New York's most notorious stock market speculators and railroad tycoons before it disappeared again into the fog.

The near-victims, Jim Fisk and Jay Gould, were fleeing not only the New York police but also the only eastern railroad mogul more powerful then they. Cornelius Vanderbilt did not take well to being flimflammed and he had been badly flimflammed by the two men in the rowboat.

In 1867, the Commodore, as Vanderbilt already was known, was just gaining control of the New York Central. He had started in the shipping business as a boy with a single sailing scow, then quickly moved to small steamers; after an internship running a friend's steamboat company, he started his own. By the 1840s his business acumen and his propensity to reinvest his profits in the purchase of more and more vessels had made him the largest shipowner in the United States—this

when he was still in his forties. In 1854 Vanderbilt reported his net worth to be about $11 million, an unheard-of fortune in those days. By that time he had moved into railroads in a big way, taking control of both the Harlem Railroad, which ran into central Manhattan, and the Hudson River Railroad, with its economical sea-level route along the Hudson River to Albany. He also held a stock interest in the fledgling New York Central, an amalgamation of nine small lines that ran between Albany and Buffalo. In less than twenty years Vanderbilt had become the dominant player in the major railroad network leading to America's largest city and greatest port.

The New York Central did have competition, of course. The Pennsylvania Railroad, using Philadelphia and Trenton and Camden and Amboy rights-of-way, reached Jersey City in 1867 and set about building waterfront terminals there and at Harsimus Cove. The Erie Railway, known as the New York and Erie until 1862, was the other major competitor. It was the first trunk line, or major long-distance carrier, in the United States, with the completion in 1852 of its tracks from New York Harbor to Lake Erie, a distance of more than five hundred miles (800km). For a time the Erie was the longest railroad in the world—and nearly the brokest. Its development had been wildly expensive, far more than even its most severe critics could have guessed. It cost $23,500,000 to build a single-track line to the Hudson, and more yet to Jersey. Nearly every source of financing, including the New York State legislature and citizens of every town on its route, had been tapped and tapped again. The Erie's treasury was bare, its soul was mortgaged to the hilt, and it flirted with bankruptcy on a nearly seasonal basis.

Interestingly enough, it was Vanderbilt himself, already on the Erie board of directors, along with Daniel Drew, an old-time stock manipulator, who was responsible for putting Jay Gould and Jim Fisk, the men who would soon rake the Commodore over the Erie coals, on the railroad's board. The two new men had taken different roads to power. Jim Fisk built a horse-and-wagon peddler route into a dry-goods empire. Jay Gould, a surveyor and tannery owner, bought the Rutland and Washington Railroad, which ran from Vermont to Troy, New York. He and Gould also learned the workings of the stock market. The New York Stock Exchange, virtually unregulated in the 1860s, was putty in the hands of wily stock manipulators who used every shady tactic to make enormous profits on their investments.

It was not long before Gould and Fisk, with the assistance of Daniel Drew, took over the Erie board and proceeded to enrich themselves by issuing nearly worthless bonds and speculating on inflated stock. Vanderbilt, who was no longer on the Erie board, was primarily interested in protecting his investment in the New York Central. Already the Pennsylvania and the Erie were cutting into the NYC's revenues, and Vanderbilt was afraid of a ruinous rate war over the freight the three railroads were carrying to and from New York. The Commodore wanted a pact among the three railroads, setting rates and pooling and dividing profits. The Pennsylvania board agreed, but to the Commodore's surprise and dismay, the Erie board turned down his proposal.

So Vanderbilt decided to buy Erie stock until he acquired a controlling interest in the railroad. The only trouble was that the more Erie stock Vanderbilt bought, the more Fisk and Gould printed. Fisk is said to have remarked, "If this printing press don't break down, I'll be damned if I don't give the old hog all he wants of Erie."

Not until Fisk and Gould had more than $7 million of the Commodore's money did Vanderbilt realize he had failed; his next tactic was to go after them in court. Since they had already violated the court's order not to issue more stock (converted from bonds), Vanderbilt had a friendly New York judge issue a citation for contempt of court. Fisk and Gould heard the news immediately: the sheriff's men would serve the contempt citation and then throw them in jail. They hurriedly left Erie's Manhattan

A Central Railroad of New Jersey steam-powered tug guides a carfloat with a boxcar-riding crewman past the Statue of Liberty, perhaps to one of the Long Island City or Bronx freight terminals or interchange yards. The small, fifty-ton (50.8t), eight-panel hoppers on the end usually carried hard coal destined for domestic consumption.

Right: The Erie Railroad's elegant Twenty-third Street Manhattan ferry terminal shortly after it was rebuilt in 1905. The Erie had been running ferries here since 1868. The CRRNJ and the Delaware, Lackawanna & Western had ferry terminals to the left, and the large plaza was a major streetcar terminus.

Above: The Atlantic Basin, Brooklyn, facing Governor's Island, circa 1903, was the equivalent of European enclosed basins for unloading ships. Constructed for handling general cargo in 1841, the basin was converted to grain handling after the steam-operated grain elevator was introduced in 1847. In the background at right is one of the original grain elevators, and in front of it are two floating grain elevators. At far right are "Brooklyn stores," nineteenth-century warehouses with rows of roof supports for hoists used to raise cargo to the upper floors. Shown is a fine selection of the barges and lighters then used. To the right of the ship are a covered lighter, then a stick lighter (with its own mast and derrick for loading), another covered lighter, and finally a self-propelled steam lighter. To the right next to the pier are a hold barge and two stick lighters. Outward is a stick lighter and a covered barge with mast and boom. By the time this photograph was taken the basin's warehouses had been converted for general cargo.

headquarters and retired to Delmonico's to consider their situation over champagne and oysters. But soon their lookouts warned that the sheriff's men were closing in. One step ahead of the law, they hailed a carriage and set off for the docks; once across the Hudson in New Jersey, outside the New York court's jurisdiction, they would be safe. Their only problem was that they could find nothing larger than a rowing skiff to take them through the swirling waters of the Hudson River to the Jersey shore.

After their close call in the rowboat that night, Fisk and Gould eventually stopped one of their own fleet of railroad-owned

Right: A freighter unloads a pallet of cartons directly onto a flatcar on a station float. Normally, ships at anchor offshore or secured to a dock while discharging on the seaward side would unload on to a lighter. However, with a station float the cartons could be landed on to a flatcar and then could be taken on hand trucks along the walkway directly to the proper refrigerator car, thus saving a substantial amount of labor.

Below: Central Railroad of New Jersey's Bronx Freight House near the Second Avenue Elevated Railroad bridge over the Harlem River. This 1944 photo amply displays CRRNJ's cramped quarters and their odd-shaped solution to it. This two-hundred-foot (60.8m) -diameter structure was copied from the design of a Harlem Transfer RR freight house built upriver in 1898. The bridges seen beyond the railroad bridge are the Willis Avenue and the Triborough Bridge's Harlem River span. To avoid having to wait for drawbridges to open, CRRNJ used the smallest of their tugs, which could pass under closed spans to deliver carfloats from their Jersey City yard.

Above: A World War II–era photograph from on top of the New York, Ontario & Western coal pier 1, where bunker coal was loaded into waiting coal-burning steamships by clamshell buckets on rail-mounted cranes. Shortly after the war, coal-fired vessels, piers 1 and 2, and the NYO&W, itself, were all obsolete and abandoned. The switcher was probably leased or borrowed from the U.S. Military Railroad Service (MRS) by the locomotive-strapped NYO&W.

Right: This 1911 photograph shows the New York, Ontario, & Western's two coal piers just north of New York Central's Weehawken Terminal. Coal brought from Pennsylvania was unloaded into barges here for harbor delivery or for loading into sailing ships. The sign on the American Cotton Oil company pier on the left advertises "Gold Dust Twins," perhaps a cleaning agent.

ferries, which deposited them in Jersey City. There they took over Taylor's Hotel. Fortifying the area with three twelve-pound cannons, they moved in more than fifty armed police, detectives, and bodyguards to prevent Vanderbilt's men from kidnapping them back to New York. Gould and Fisk had beat the legend. They would be the only ones to do so, and what's more, they would even do it again.

By 1870 the Erie, the Pennsylvania, and the Central all had completed lines to Chicago and were in the midst of a freight-rate war, lowering their rates for transporting various commodities, principally livestock, to New York. The price for moving a carload of cattle dropped from $120 to $40. Then the Erie lowered its rate to one dollar per carload. Vanderbilt, knowing that his Central was financially far stronger than the other road, did likewise, but he was surprised to see that while his trains were transporting huge numbers of cattle (nearly for free, of course), the Erie was carrying almost none. Too late did Vanderbilt discover that Fisk and Gould had cornered the cattle market in eastern New York—buying more than six thousand animals. Gleefully, they put their herds on Vanderbilt's railroad in Buffalo and, thanks to the Commodore's generosity,

The famous steamer *Commonwealth* passes in front of the Hell Gate Bridge in 1939. The Hell Gate was considered the nastiest stretch of water in Long Island Sound, with currents so strong that the bridge had to be constructed by cranes working from each bank rather than by barge-mounted cranes anchored midstream. A Baldwin-Westinghouse EP-2 electric brings a New Haven passenger train into Manhattan, passing a steam-led freight. The luxurious *Commonwealth*, at 456 feet (138.6m) the largest inland water steamer in America, was built by William Cramp & Sons in Philadelphia in 1908. Able to carry more than one thousand passengers and six hundred tons (609.6t) of freight, she was a side-wheeler with great maneuverability, and her 11,000hp compound engine gave her a maximum speed of 23 miles (36.8km) per hour. She was called the "Queen of the Sound" and by some wags "Mellen's apartment house" (Charles Mellen was then president of the New Haven Railroad and the Fall River Line).

sold them in New York for handsome profits. After that, the fuming Vanderbilt would have nothing further to do with Gould, Fisk, or the Erie.

More and more railroads built tracks or acquired rights-of-way to New York Harbor. The Lackawanna came in 1868. In the early 1870s the Lehigh Valley Railroad began moving coal from Pennsylvania to a Jersey City coal terminal, and the Ontario and Western completed a line from Oswego, New York. In 1883 the Baltimore and Ohio acquired rights to the Central of New Jersey's line to Jersey City, then bought Staten Island Rapid

Transit to develop a waterfront yard at St. George, opposite the south end of Manhattan. The Philadelphia and Reading came in 1892, establishing a coal terminal on the Jersey side of Arthur Kill, one of seven coal terminals located around the harbor.

One of the least viable of the newcomers was the New York, West Shore, and Buffalo, known as the West Shore. With a route that paralleled the Central's to Buffalo, in late 1883 it began passenger service from Albany to a waterfront terminal situated at Weehawken, New Jersey, just across the Hudson from central Manhattan. Immediately it fell into a disastrous rate war with Vanderbilt's Central. Passenger fares and freight rates were pushed so low that the Central

was losing a fortune and the West Shore was teetering on the edge of bankruptcy.

The backers of the West Shore were a varied bunch who had no love for Vanderbilt. George Pullman was said to be unhappy that Vanderbilt had opted for Wagner Palace cars instead of Pullman's sleepers. Pennsylvania Railroad investors aimed to slow down the growth of their arch-rival, the Central, and retaliate against Vanderbilt's financing of a competing road running between Philadelphia and Pittsburgh—right in their very backyard—the South Penn RR. Foreign investors, represented by J.P. Morgan's banks, also had large sums at stake.

Morgan became concerned that the ruinous competition would disrupt the financial markets and discourage foreign investment. In 1885 he called the warring parties to a meeting on his yacht, the *Corsair*, and informed the gentlemen that they would not likely set foot on shore again until they resolved their dispute. And resolve it they did: the PRR took over the South Penn, and Vanderbilt acquired the West Shore. Although Vanderbilt neither wanted nor needed it at the time, he would soon enough be thankful to have it.

By 1900 the amount of freight carried on American railroads had increased dramatically, and railroad freight shipments into or through New York Harbor had skyrocketed. The Central could no longer operate all its freight yards in increasingly congested Manhattan. So freight destined to be loaded onto vessels was sent to the old West Shore yards at Weehawken, New Jersey—now greatly expanded—where it was transferred to lighters. Thus, the little West Shore became one of the most important New York Harbor fixtures and Vanderbilt's forced investment paid New York Central dividends a thousandfold.

While many railroads had come to New York Harbor, only a select few had rights-of-way into New York's sweetest kernel—the island of Manhattan. Throughout the nineteenth century Vanderbilt's Central had sole entry to Manhattan, crossing the Harlem River at Spuyten Duyvil on a bridge originally built by the Hudson River Railroad (at Manhattan's north tip). Not until 1910 would the Pennsylvania Railroad complete its tunnel under the Hudson River from Weehawken to the new Pennsylvania Station at Seventh Avenue and Thirty-third Street. Seven years later the PRR and the New Haven opened the Hell's Gate Bridge over the East River, linking Manhattan with Long Island and allowing

Getting up steam. Part of New York Central's tug fleet awaits crews after overnight servicing at the Weehawken, New Jersey, maintenance facility. The tank in the foreground is for steam cleaning, and the used-tire fenders replaced the old handwoven collision mats that previously had been made by the crews and by the partially disabled. New York Central had the last fleet of steam tugs in the harbor and used them until 1967. *No. 34*, center, is one of only two diesel-powered tugs in New York Central's fleet in this 1940s scene. Note the high pilot-houses, so built to allow visibility over the tops of boxcars on carfloats. Besides their regular work, tugs often assisted ferryboats during the winter when the harbor became heavily iced.

through-rail service from the south via New York City to Boston and other cities in New England. Previously, the New Haven's predecessor, the New York and New England Railroad, had bought the railroad-car ferry *Maryland*, 238 feet (72.3m) and 1,150 gross tons (1,168.4t), built originally in 1853 to ferry trains across the Susquehanna River between Philadelphia and Baltimore. The New Haven used her to move entire passenger trains (and their passengers) from Boston to Philadelphia, Washington, D.C., and other points south, connecting a railhead in the Bronx via the East River to a railhead in Jersey City.

In addition to providing facilities for its own passenger trains, the PRR's Penn Station also was the terminal for the Long

Above: In a Manhattan scene from the 1920s, we see the Fall River Line's steamers *New Hampshire* and *Providence* alongside their North River dock at the foot of Fulton Street. In the background is the huge World Telegram Building. To the right is the freight boat *Yale* of the Starin-New Haven Line. The vessel *New Hampshire*, in the foreground, made overnight runs to New London, where passengers could transfer to the Central Vermont Railway for connections to both Vermont and New Hampshire. Behind the *New Hampshire* the side-wheeler *Providence* loads coal from a barge. The Fall River vessels' main operations were between New York and Norwich, Stonington, Providence, Newport, and Fall River.

Opposite top: The PRR tug *Philadelphia* docked in front of the Whitehall Building at 17 Battery Place. For many years the Morgan Tug Company, one of New York's largest tug fleets, had its headquarters in the Whitehall Building; from a high ledge on this building, before the era of radio-telephone systems in vessels, chief dispatcher Captain Dan Anglim would scream his orders through a six-foot (1.8m) megaphone to the company's tugs docked across Battery Place. One of the *Philadelphia*'s main duties was towing coal barges. She was a 1,600hp diesel-electric built by RTC Shipbuilding for the PRR, which pioneered the use of diesel-engine tugs.

The 110-foot (33.4m) boat could be controlled by her crew from the after-deck, allowing the captain to assist with hawsers if need be. New York's railroad-owned tug crews were considered railroad men, not mariners.

Opposite bottom: Two Long Island Railroad tugs idle at the railroad's Long Island City floatbridge on a slow day in the early 1950s. The Long Island Railroad shared carfloat interchange facilities with both the Pennsy and the New Haven railroads. The little Long Island Railroad alone had more than seventy carfloats, tugs, ferries, and other craft; the Pennsy had more than three hundred; and the New Haven probably had more than 150 vessels. The 107-foot (31.7m) *Garden City*, a steam tug in the diesel era, was built by Pusey & Jones in Wilmington, Delaware, in 1941 and was powered by an 800hp Skinner Uniflo. Next to her is the *Meitowax*, a 680hp diesel built in 1925 that, after being sold in 1963, sank off Cape Hatteras while being transferred south to her new owners. The floatbridge operated by a gantry lowering or raising the apron or bridge until it connected with the carfloat. Then bolts would be driven through holes in the apron into sockets on the carfloat to secure it. The bridgeman directed the operation from a console in the small house next to the *Garden City*'s wheelhouse.

At the Bronx Terminal Market longshoremen load bananas on a PRR station float, also called an umbrella float because of its central canopy. A cop stands by, watching to see that no bananas or refrigerator cars are pilfered. The station floats allowed electric or gas mules (that is, tractors) to tow trailers right into boxcars or reefers, greatly expediting the movement of cargo. The Bronx Towing Company's wooden tug *Helen Buchanan*, built in 1902, waits to take the carfloat in tow. It was not only railroad tugs that moved railroad floats and lighters around the harbor, though independent towing was not a common occurrence. In the background are the 145th Street Bridge, spanning the Harlem River, and, to the right, barges, one loaded with coal.

Island, Lehigh Valley, and some New Haven trains, along with, in later years, limiteds of the Atlantic Coast Line, Seaboard Air Line, Southern Railway, Norfolk and Western, and the Chesapeake and Ohio. The New York Central's Grand Central Terminal handled all that road's New York City passenger traffic as well as many of the New Haven's and, later, trains from the Boston and Albany, Boston and Maine, Delaware and Hudson, and other roads. All this notwithstanding, most Manhattan-bound railroad passengers made their entrance by water.

All the other lines that wished to reach America's most important passenger destination were forced to develop mar-

itime transportation systems. The Central Railroad of New Jersey shared a Jersey City terminal and ferryboats with the Reading Company. The Baltimore and Ohio, to get a piece of the Manhattan pie, also used Jersey Central's terminal, boarding passengers on buses (from the 1920s onward), which were in turn carried by the Jersey Central auto ferries. The Erie had its own Jersey City terminal and ferry system, which was also used by the New York, Susquehanna, and Western. The Lackawanna's terminal was just north at Hoboken, from which it moved through-trains, locals, and also freights. Finally, at Weehawken, opposite Manhattan's Forty-second Street, the West Shore Railroad—later the River Division of the New York Central—operated a terminal that it shared with the New York, Ontario, and Western.

Although passenger traffic into New York was extremely important, it was only a small part of the railroads' maritime operations. Not only did the seven million residents of Manhattan have to be fed, clothed, and supplied, but enormous quantities of cargo had to move in and out of the world's biggest port, and there simply was no way to do it except by

Right: Southern Pacific's Morgan Lines/Atlantic S.S. Company piers on the North River in Manhattan in the 1930s. Atlantic Steamship was an important coastal shipping company. It occupied five adjacent piers, scheduled five or six passenger and/or freight sailings a week, and maintained its own small barge fleet.

Below: Looking toward New York Central's Sixtieth Street Manhattan yard and piers from its Weehawken, New Jersey, yard about 1950. In the foreground locomotives bound for export are being loaded aboard the ship at left. Floating cranes unload ore from the vessel at right into rail cars. The covered hoppers, foreground, probably wait to load bauxite ore, which needs to be protected from the weather.

water. With the exception of the New York Central, no railroad had freight routes into Manhattan, and even the Central's were very limited. True, docks lined both the Brooklyn shore and the Jersey side of the Hudson, but most of the oceangoing vessels entering New York Harbor berthed at one of the more than one hundred and fifty piers in Lower Manhattan, though many were for the use of the railroads. So how was the immense amount of freight moved around New York Harbor?

Let us take a typical mixed-freight arriving from, say, Chicago in the 1920s. Likely she would belong to one of the trunk lines. If she was a New York Central, she would probably head into the Central's North Bergen classification yard. If she was an Erie train, she would go to Croxton, and if she belonged to the Pennsylvania Railroad, to their Meadows yard; all these huge yards lay two or three miles (3.2–4.8km) west of the Jersey waterfront. Freight trains arriving from New England would be assigned to one of the Bronx or Brooklyn yards for classification.

Once in the classification yard the train's cars would be separated by destination. Freight cars slated to be unloaded alongside Jersey-berthed vessels would be shunted to their piers. Cars bound for Manhattan or its docks, for Bronx or Brooklyn delivery, or for seaside loading of vessels docked in Jersey, would be loaded on carfloats at waterfront rail yards, then moved by tug to their destinations. The Erie, carrying more than 90 percent of New York's fruit and vegetables and much of its dairy products, floated them from the Jersey City and Weehawken yards across the Hudson to a number of piers on Manhattan's lower west side. The New York Central's main car float terminal was also at Weehawken, while the Penn's largest waterfront yards were further south at Bayonne

Above: The venerable Pennsylvania Railroad twin-screw steamer *Elisha Lee* was originally built as the *Richard Peck* in 1892 for the New Haven Line and ran to New Haven and Providence before being transferred to another of the New Haven Railroad's steamship companies, the New England S.S. Company. In 1937, with the collapse of the Fall River Line, she was sold to a sightseeing company and later taken over by the U.S. Navy in World War II. Then after being renovated and renamed, she joined the Pennsy Railroad's subsidiary, the New York, Philadelphia & Norfolk's Cape Charles-to-Norfolk service, until she was laid up in 1953. She was considered to be one of the most popular Long Island steamers ever to sail.

Left: A freight consist hauled by a GG-1 flashes by the deserted PRR Wilmington, Delaware, station early on Christmas morning during the early 1950s. Idling at the station is a Baldwin Shark Nose diesel making one of PRR's many daily passenger runs on the busy coastal corridor between Washington, D.C., and New York. The GG-1 was designed by the famous architect and industrial designer Raymond Loewy in 1934. Loewy, whose initial job for the railroad was to design the garbage cans at Penn Station, wound up designing such other locomotive classics as the S-1, the T-1, and the streamlined K-4.

Much of the freight from the train would be transferred at the Jersey yards onto lighters (barges), which would subsequently be unloaded at other waterfront locations or alongside ships. This included much of the "package," or less-than-carload (LCL), freight, which was sorted at special freight houses, known as pier stations, before being loaded onto freight cars that were then placed on railroad-car barges, known as carfloats. The railroad cars were then moved to their destinations, which might be any of the thousands of manufacturing plants located around New York Harbor. LCL freight destined for export was usually put onto lighters alongside a pier or was loaded directly onto a vessel. Cargo unloaded from arriving vessels went through the process in reverse.

Maritime railroad operations in New York Harbor started before the Civil War, when independent companies contracted to provide lighters to the railroads. The Pennsylvania was the first railroad to own and operate its own fleet, in 1879. Before long the other major railroads were in the business as well, most of them with extensive fleets and facilities. By 1885 New York Central was operating ninety-two vessels to and from piers in Jersey, on the east and west sides of Manhattan, and in Brooklyn

Opposite: The Central Railroad of New Jersey's Jersey City yard, with lower Manhattan in the background. In the center is CRRNJ's passenger station and ferry terminal, and to the right are lighterage piers and floatbridges for loading cars onto carfloats. The photo was taken in the late 1940s or early 1950s.

Below: A mid-1940s view of the Hudson River and Manhattan, with, in the foreground, the New Jersey waterfront terminals of (left to right) the Delaware, Lackawanna & Western, the Erie, and the Pennsylvania railroads. The finger piers running along both shores and the working watercraft bustling around the harbor became obsolete not long after this photograph was taken.

and the Bronx. The Pennsylvania Railroad had 104 vessels, and the Erie nearly that many. By the 1920s the Pennsylvania's and the New York Central's fleets had tripled in size, and three other railroads had more than two hundred vessels each. In 1946 the Erie operated 111 covered barges, eighty-two lighters (of which five were self-propelled), twenty-six carfloats, twelve tugs, and five ferries, all crewed and maintained by more than 670 men. Besides the railroad-owned operations, there were four independent terminals in Brooklyn: the Bush Terminal, the New York Dock, the Jay Street Connecting, and the Eastern District Terminal, which supplied both switching and carfloat services to the railroads and had their own small fleets.

The "railroad navies," as they became known, were a service predicated on cheap labor, but to build, maintain, and operate these imposing fleets began to be astronomically expensive. By the 1950s railroads were delivering more and more goods by truck, operating on a greatly expanded system of newly built highways, bridges, and tunnels. By 1965 containerization was a fact, and the enormous Port Newark–Elizabeth (New Jersey) container facility was already under construction. It would replace virtually all of New York Harbor's break-bulk (or piecemeal) loading and unloading and would render superfluous nearly all of the marine rail operations. Today, only the Cross Harbor Railroad, successor to the four Brooklyn terminals, still operates a few carfloats across a nearly empty New York Harbor.

A 1924 view of the Delaware, Lackawanna & Western's Hoboken, New Jersey, waterfront facilities on the Hudson River. To the left is the DL&W's coal dumping pier and covered freight piers. In the center is the railroad's passenger station and ferry terminal for Manhattan-bound passengers. To the right are the Hoboken Piers and behind them is the city of Hoboken. Bergen Hill, a major barrier to railroads attempting to reach the waterfront, lies in the background.

Right: As a means of delivering goods to Manhattan, railroads whose tracks terminated in New Jersey would load boxcars filled with Manhattan-bound goods on station floats and tow them to "pier stations" such as the one pictured here in 1944. These, mostly along the Hudson and East rivers, would be accessible by drays. Goods would be wheeled out of the cars, down the platforms, and into sheds or directly into the waiting consignee's trucks.

Above: A view of lower Manhattan in 1924 as seen from the Hudson River, with the East River and the Manhattan Bridge in the background. Left center are the Pennsylvania Railroad's Cortland Street ferry and the CRRNJ's Liberty Street ferry. To the right are pier stations with carfloats alongside. Freight was loaded or unloaded from the freight cars without the need to run tracks throughout overbuilt Manhattan. In the first half of the twentieth century, between two thousand and three thousand freight cars were floated to and from Manhattan pier stations every day. The Woolworth building, in the center, was then the tallest building in the world.

THE PORT OF NEW YORK AUTHORITY

NEW YORK HARBOR

TERMINALS

SCALE IN FEET

Opposite: A map of the "world's greatest port" in 1949 that shows railroad float yards and railroad-owned marine terminals.

Top: With the Brooklyn Eastern District Terminal Railroad's steam tug *Invincible* looking on, *No.10*, a Porter 0-6-0 tank, switches cars at the BEDT's main Kent Street Yards. The BEDT, which was reorganized from a small predecessor in 1906, was one of the four small independent terminal railways serving Brooklyn. With the loss of traffic in the 1980s it merged with the New York Dock Railway to form the harbor's last carfloat operation, the New York Cross Harbor. This photograph predates the 1962 scrapping of *No.10* and the demise of the BEDT's six other Porters and its steam tugs. In the background is the Williamsburg Bridge.

Center: The Erie Lackawanna ferry *Elmira* makes her way from the railroad's Hoboken terminal to Manhattan in this 1963 photo. The *Elmira* was built in 1905 by Newport News Ship Building and was the last steam ferry to operate for the Delaware, Lackawanna & Western. She continued running after that railroad's merger with the Erie in 1960. The *Elmira*'s last run was in 1967.

Bottom: New York Central's ferry *Weehawken* laid up at the railroad's Weehawken Terminal, probably in the early 1960s. The *Weehawken* carried mostly commuters on the West Shore run to Forty-second Street. The ferry was built by Harlan and Hollingsworth in 1914. To the right, behind the boxcars, is a New York Central floatbridge.

CHAPTER TWO

THE GREAT LAKES

Some "whirlies" at work. These small (often rail-mounted and self-propelled) steam cranes were nicknamed
"whirlies" because of their ability to rapidly rotate. They were one of the first mechanized means of
unloading coal and other materials, as seen in this photograph, taken circa 1885. The schooner-rigged vessel
shown unloading on the Cuyahoga River is a remnant of sail in an increasingly steam-powered world.

The Great Lakes

By the time the first railroad came into Chicago from New York over the Northern Indiana's tracks in 1852, the Windy City was already a major port. In fact, Chicago had become the most important port west of New York. The hundred-mile (160km) -long Illinois and Michigan Canal had opened in 1848, linking the Illinois River (a part of the Mississippi system) with the Chicago River, which led to Lake Michigan. Suddenly, Chicago was the apex of a river system running to the Gulf and a lake/canal system leading all the way to the East Coast (eight ice-free months a year).

Small paddle-wheelers brought grain, hogs, and produce to Chicago from thousands of farms recently established in areas adjacent to the Mississippi in Iowa, southern Illinois, and Missouri. Lake traffic also grew. By 1849 a dozen palatial side-wheel steamers, as large as a thousand tons (1,016t), operated regular passenger schedules between Chicago and Buffalo, stopping at Milwaukee en route. Many smaller steamers, including the new propeller-driven screw-steamers, and numerous sailing craft, mostly schooners, plied the lakes carrying wheat, flour, timber, livestock, and produce to cities in the East and manufactured goods and coal to the West.

Chicago's population exploded. In 1837 the city had only four thousand residents. Ten years later that number had reached sixteen thousand. By 1860 the city was home to 109,000 people, and by 1900 Chicago's population had soared

What had started as an afterthought for the Illinois Central—laying tracks into Chicago—paid for itself in less than a decade as Chicago rapidly developed into the greatest metropolis in the Midwest. Within a few years the railroad yards were expanded in front of the enormous Michigan Avenue townhouses in the background; the homeowners who were, no doubt, all railroad fans, must have been enchanted with their new view of Chicago's "railroad avenue."

to nearly 1,700,000. The numbers continued to increase dramatically through the early twentieth century. The port grew as well. By the mid-1850s Chicago was handling more vessels per day than the country's next six busiest ports, including New York's (though Chicago's tonnage numbers, in terms of both the size of vessels and the amount of cargo, never approximated New York's).

In 1855 the Sault Sainte Marie Canals opened, connecting Lake Superior to the other lakes, and that same year funds were allocated to dredge the channel between Lake Huron and Lake Erie. By 1858 more than fifteen hundred vessels (but carrying only 400,000 total tons [406,400t]) plied the Great Lakes. Shipping's supremacy would be short-lived, however: the railroads' threat was just around the corner.

But no steamship man could have felt threatened (except perhaps about the safety of his horses) that day in 1848 when the Galena and Chicago Union's *Pioneer*, a spindly little 4-2-0, lurched off from Chicago's riverfront on its inaugural run with much huffing and puffing and whistle-blowing. Chicago's first railroad tracks had just been laid to Oak Park, a grand seven miles (11.2km) away. Of the company's directors and the civic leaders in the single coach rattling and swaying behind the *Pioneer*, one would soon be famous as the Midwest's greatest railroad baron.

The Great Central Depot, built in 1853 at the cost of $250,000, was used by the Illinois Central, the Michigan Central, and the Chicago, Burlington & Quincy. Beyond the railroad right-of-way is the mouth of the Chicago River and the entrance to Chicago's harbor, with grain elevators in the background. The lagoon eventually was filled in with debris from the Great Chicago Fire of 1871.

William Butler Ogden, though an easterner, was taken with Chicago and sensed its potential for growth. Shortly after taking up residence there, he became the newly incorporated town's first mayor. He also traveled the lanes by horse and buggy between Chicago and Galena, on the Mississippi, selling stock for the Galena line (which, by the way, would never reach Galena). Once that railroad was operating, he helped to develop the Pittsburgh, Fort Wayne, and Chicago, a railroad that he hoped would compete with the Erie Canal and Great Lakes steamships as a direct link between Chicago and the East. Then Ogden's eyes traveled westward toward Wisconsin and Minnesota and their great timber and iron ore reserves. He bought the Chicago and Milwaukee Railroad, which had just been completed, connecting the two cities.

With both eastern and midwestern financial backing, Ogden began buying up other railroads throughout a four-state area. One of these, then only partially built, would connect Chicago with Green Bay, via Pig's Eye, on the northern Mississippi. Pig's Eye was to become St. Paul, and the Chicago, St. Paul, and Fond

Chicago's Union Station was built in 1881 by the Pittsburgh, Fort Wayne & Chicago and the Pittsburgh, Cincinnati, Chicago & St. Louis, both of which were controlled by the Pennsylvania Railroad. The crowd gathered in front of the station, close to the lakefront, is likely involved in the Burlington strike of February 27, 1888, by the Brotherhood of Locomotive Engineers. The Union Station, later known as the Pennsylvania Station, was replaced in 1925 by the present Union Station, home to Amtrak and Metra (the local rail commuter line).

du Lac Railroad would be merged with the Galena and Chicago Union in 1864 to form the Chicago and North Western. This line established Chicago as the linchpin of midwestern rail transport and the center of Ogden's railroad network, spanning more than 860 miles (1376km). Ogden was already the first president of the fledgling Union Pacific. With its Central Pacific connection and Ogden's Chicago and North Western, in 1869 the Union Pacific became part of the country's first transcontinental railroad to San Francisco—via Chicago, of course.

As much as Ogden relished dominating Chicago's entire railroad network, he could not. Some of the bitterest railroad battles in the nation were taking place between the many lines desperate for a presence there, and no single railroad could gain total control. Fate and luck were to play almost as great a role as power and money in awarding keys to the city.

The Illinois Central (IC), a land-grant railroad that was building main lines mostly from north to south in the state, at first only wanted a branch line into Chicago. Even at that the directors found their route neatly blocked by the Chicago and Rock Island, which had joined with the Michigan Southern and the Northern Indiana railroads to buy vital Chicago land that gave them access to downtown. Immediately the combine had laid tracks across the Illinois Central's projected route.

Thwarted, but more determined than ever to enter the city, in 1852 the IC's directors ordered a line built along Lake Michigan five miles (8km) south of the city to run north along the lake to Twenty-third Street, then Chicago's outer limit. So far, so good—but would the city fathers allow the line to continue along the lake, destroying what had become Chicago's most fashionable neighborhood and the city's most scenic vistas? Well, yes, maybe they would, if the IC agreed to build out into the lake, then dam and shore up their right-of-way, thus protecting a fast-eroding shoreline that the city had not been financially able to maintain. The Central agreed. In return for the city's "gift" of a 300-foot (912m) -wide easement that was actually in the lake, it would build dikes and breakwaters and maintain them to safeguard the IC's tracks and the city's shoreline.

Initially the cost of building the lake route nearly drained the Illinois Central, but the choice eventually proved to be a bonanza. The land flanking the IC's tracks south of Chicago became one of the greatest industrial areas in America and provided the railroad with astounding freight revenues.

The Illinois Central had allied itself with and provided trackage rights to one of Michigan's two fierce railroad competitors, the Michigan Central (MC). The combined IC/MC entrance into the Chicago area caused one of America's celebrated "crossing-frog wars," with some terrible consequences. Since the Rock Island/Michigan Southern tracks had been laid

first, the IC/MC found that at some point it needed to cross them to gain entrance to its route along the lake. Of course the Rock Island/Michigan Southern denied permission to their arch-rival and posted a guard at the point where they expected the IC/MC to try and cross. One night Illinois Central henchmen kidnapped the guard, and the next morning a fine-looking crossing frog was found neatly installed.

Both railroad combines pretended the crossing didn't exist. They ran their trains over it with reckless abandon until the sad day in 1853 when the inevitable train wreck killed eighteen people. As a result, a new Illinois law forced all trains approaching a crossing to come to a complete stop before proceeding. The feud, which was more between the two Michigan railroads than between the Rock Island and the IC, was pointless anyway. Not only did both railroads reach their goal and develop profitable routes, but soon they were both taken over by the grasping Cornelius Vanderbilt's New York Central, along with the Indiana Southern and a half-dozen other lines. The Commodore

The Illinois Central retained control of its valuable downtown Chicago right-of-way. An Illinois Central passenger train heads out of the city in this early 1950s photograph taken from the IC's office tower next to its Twelfth Street, or "Central," Station. To the right are the tracks for the IC's electrified suburban service. Built over the tracks is the Chicago Art Institute and to the far right, just out of the picture, is Lake Michigan.

The Atchison, Topeka & Santa Fe's Corwith freight yard, five miles (8km) west of Dearborn Station, had a capacity of 5,871 freight cars. The longest track held 106 cars. And this was just one of many enormous rail yards around Chicago. When this photo was taken, in the early 1960s, the Chicago area boasted twenty trunk-line railroads that operated close to one-half the nation's total railroad mileage, according to *Chicago* magazine. The large building on the left is a car-repair shed.

the Chicago-New York route, then plainly seen as the most important and potentially lucrative in the country.

Of course nearly every railroad in America had at least the dream of connecting with Chicago—and many made it. By 1860 there were already eleven lines into the city, and the number continued to grow. The Alton came from St. Louis. The Green Bay, Milwaukee, and Chicago arrived in 1855. The Chicago, Milwaukee, and St. Paul forged another link to the west, and one day would run all the way to the Pacific. The Pittsburgh, Fort Wayne, and Chicago Railway ran in the oppo-

site direction, joining the three cities in 1858 and coming under the control of the Pennsylvania Railroad eleven years later. The Baltimore and Ohio arrived, mostly on its own tracks, in 1874, from Washington, D.C., and Baltimore. The Erie eventually staggered in, as did the New York, Chicago, and St. Louis (later known as the Nickel Plate Road), the Grand Trunk Western and the Soo from Canada. In 1888 the Santa Fe made its link, and finally in 1892, so did the Wabash from Detroit and Toledo, with connections to St. Louis. By the 1890s more than thirty railroads were represented in the Chicago area.

The first railroad to operate a steamship on the Great Lakes was the predecessor of the Erie Railroad. In 1852 the New York and Erie established the Union Steamboat Company, running fourteen chartered package freighters and passenger vessels from Chicago, Toledo, and other ports to the railroad's northern terminus at Dunkirk, New York. The Erie, however, had only a few years before it faced major competition.

The Western Transit Company, the predecessor of the New York Central's Great Lakes fleet, arrived on the scene in 1855. Some of its early steamers, such as the *Queen of the West* (324 feet [98.5m], 1,851 tons [1880.6t]), were some of the most luxurious vessels sailing anywhere in the world until the "luxury liner" started crossing the Atlantic in the 1880s. By 1863 Western Transit was running ten combination passenger/package freighters between Chicago, Detroit, Cleveland, and Buffalo. Not only did Commodore Vanderbilt operate his own vessels, he also had tie-ins with the two competitors, the Michigan Central Railroad and the Michigan Southern/Northern Indiana combine, both of which ran boats from Detroit and Toledo to meet the Commodore's trains at Buffalo.

Where the New York Central ventured, its arch-rival, the Pennsylvania Railroad, could not help following. In 1867 the Pennsy entered a combine to form the Anchor Line, which ran package freighters and some quite luxurious passenger vessels between Buffalo, Chicago, and Duluth.

Other railroads also had large fleets. The Lehigh Valley Railroad established a shipping subsidiary in 1881, which operated six wooden bulk carriers and seven steel package freighters, mostly between Chicago and Buffalo. The Delaware, Lackawanna, and Western, the Central of Vermont (later the Rutland Railroad), and subsidiaries of two Canadian roads (the Great Western and the Grand Trunk), as well as a number of smaller railroads, were also active in Great Lakes shipping.

Where there had been synergy between railroads and shipping before the Civil War, with railroads depending on lake vessels to take their freight and passengers to destinations outside their short-line route systems, this quickly changed after the

This 1895 view shows the package freighter *W.H. Gratwick* discharging manufactured goods at Northern Pacific's freight shed no. 4 while one of Northern Steamship's boats sits on the outside dock. Northern Steamship was a Great Northern steamship subsidiary. The dock pictured is just inside the canal on Duluth's downtown waterfront. Great Northern boxcars are beyond the shed. Other NP docks are at left. Behind the coal dock to the right is "Elevator Row," a line of grain elevators all built since the success of the first one twenty-five years earlier. Another railroad maintaining large dock facilities, and an important ore and coal carrier, was the Duluth & Iron Range, now a U.S. Steel subsidiary known as the Duluth, Missabe & Iron Railway. Burlington Northern, an amalgamation of Northern Pacific, Great Northern, and many other roads, also maintained large loading facilities from the 1930s to the 1960s.

Shown here in 1875, the Lake Superior & Mississippi Railway dock, just outside Duluth, Minnesota's present harbor, was completed in 1870 along with the railroad's Elevator A. The first shipment of grain from Duluth was loaded from the elevator into a vessel that year. The following year the completion of the Duluth Ship Canal opened the inner harbor to shipping. The Lake Superior & Mississippi Railway ran to St. Paul, and eventually connected with the Northern Pacific network. Duluth would soon be one of the country's greatest bulk-shipping ports, moving grain and iron ore east and receiving coal.

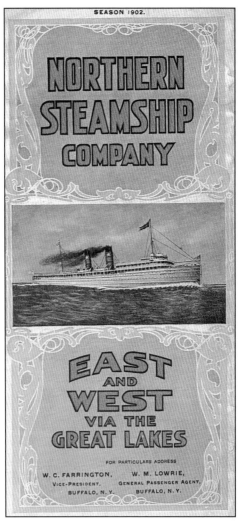

The Northern Steamship Company, the Great Northern Railway's Great Lakes subsidiary, operated two passenger vessels between Duluth, Minnesota, and Buffalo, New York, stopping at Sault Ste. Marie, Mackinac, Detroit, and Cleveland. The *North West* made a weekly round-trip commencing in 1894; it was joined a year later by the sister ship *North Land*. Each had a capacity of five hundred passengers. The brochure on the left promotes the company's east-west route. The middle brochure, undated, promises "In all the world no trip like this," perhaps a bit of hyperbole. In the right-hand brochure, the line touts the 1904 World's Fair in St. Louis, though why passengers should use the company's vessels to get there is unclear. The vessel pictured on all three brochures is the *North West*.

war was over. Railroads amalgamated and built through-routes, or trunk lines, between major cities. And the locomotive developed to the point that, by 1890, it was a powerful and speedy workhorse capable of hauling long and heavy trains for days instead of hours. Shipping companies and railroads rapidly became competitors instead of partners.

The first major shifts toward railroad domination occurred in passenger traffic and package freight. Railroads could speed their customers or their goods from Chicago to New York in two days rather than in weeks. Sleeping cars became available, though not dining cars (trains still had to make meal stops). As each year passed the railroads took more and more commodities from the shipping companies. By the 1870s, for instance, the railroads had replaced ships as the main movers of bagged flour

Right: The *North Land* and the *North West*, Northern Steamship's twins, both built by the Globe Iron Works at Cleveland in 1893 and 1894, respectively, were 386 feet (117.3m) long, had twin triple-expansion engines together producing 7,000hp, and were capable of a cruising speed of 22 mph (35.2kph). Unfortunately, the vessels, though considered to be among the most beautiful on the lakes, were extremely expensive to operate and would come to be known as "Jim Hill's White Elephants."

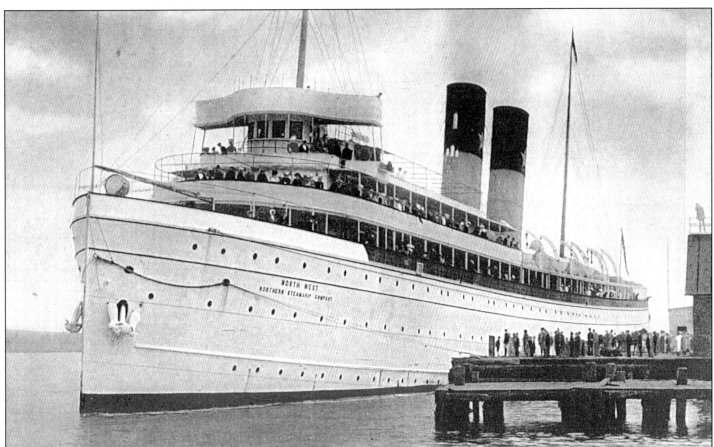

Above: The *North West*, near an unidentified dock, was originally built with three stacks, like her sister, the *North Land*. But in 1902 she was rebuilt and a larger deckhouse was added in place of the forward stack. She was damaged by fire in 1911, rebuilt as a freighter, and eventually lost in World War II. The *North Land* was broken up in Quebec in 1921. Both vessels were extremely popular with their passengers. Besides the passenger vessels, Northern Steamship ran six iron package freighters: the *Northern Wave*, *Northern Light*, *Northern King*, *Northern Queen*, *North Star*, and *North Wind*.

to the east, mostly because of flour's perishable nature and the railroads' better handling facilities. One-third of Milwaukee's flour went by rail in 1866, but by 1873 two-thirds of it did. Usually grain was still shipped by vessel, particularly after the steam-operated grain elevator (which enabled the rapid loading and discharging of huge bulk cargoes) became a part of nearly every major port. Iron ore and timber traveled predominantly on the lakes, but coal more and more moved by rail. Higher, sometimes even exorbitant, railroad freight rates, however, kept the railroads from getting an even larger share of freight traffic. In 1873 competition between rail and shipping was about even. Thereafter, railroads hauled the lion's share of freight, though not of all commodities.

By 1870 there were too many Great Lakes vessels competing for the available freight and passengers. To reduce duplication, the Erie's Union Steamboat, the Pennsylvania's Anchor Line, and the New York Central's Western Transportation Company pooled many of their Lake Superior vessels, forming the jointly owned Lake Superior Transportation Company. The company, amazingly, lasted two decades, operating twenty-one steamers at its peak. But in 1892 Lake Superior Transportation was dissolved, and its vessels were returned to their railroad owners. The railroads then continued their competition unabated until 1915, when the

In this painting, entitled *The Oriental Limited—A Vision Realized*, by O.E. Hake, James Hill is depicted as the visionary dreaming of a railway-steamship line spanning the world. James Hill was one of America's great transportation visionaries, and his railroad and steamship lines, if they did not span the world, crossed most of the North American continent and all of the Pacific Ocean—to Asia. He did have a remarkable vision, and from it he created a remarkable empire.

Right: Early 1900s Buffalo, in this postcard photo, shows plumes of coal smoke rising from all sides. Northern Steamship's *North West*, guided by a tug, slowly moves out of the narrow mouth of the Buffalo River (and the entrance to Buffalo's harbor) as it departs on one of its weekly sailings. On the end of the man-made South Pier, constructed to protect the harbor, sits *China Light*, built in 1883. The large building in the background on the right is the Union Elevator, owned by the Delaware, Lackawanna & Western, and the tower at left is part of the City and County Hall.

Above: Substantial changes took place in Buffalo Harbor in the thirty-six years between the previous photograph and this one. This 1924 photo shows the ship canal at left with, near its mouth, the connecting terminal elevator. The elevator and the connecting terminal railroad were both owned by the Pennsylvania Railroad. On the right bank of the Buffalo River is the passenger terminal (and Hoboken counterpart) of the Delaware, Lackawanna & Western. Behind the second vessel from the river's mouth is the road's freight house. At the tip of land extending into the lake is DL&W's coal-loading facility, an important asset that allowed the anthracite road to ship to locations far removed from its rail system. By 1907, Lackawanna's subsidiary, the Lake Transit Company, with its fleet of eight package freighters, had been disbanded and the vessels sold. The company had operated on the Great Lakes since the early 1880s.

Top right: The Anchor Line, also known as the Erie & Western Transportation Company, a Pennsylvania Railroad subsidiary, had been involved in Great Lakes shipping since 1867. In 1871 it had three famous passenger-freighters built: the *China*, *India*, and *Japan*. A fourth vessel, the *Alaska*, carried no passengers. The *Octorara*, pictured in the brochure, was the last of three palatial passenger vessels, all built between 1903 and 1909. These ships and seventeen others built for the Anchor Line from the middle 1870s, mostly package freighters, all carried names of Pennsylvania rivers. The line lasted until 1915.

Top far right: The officers of the *Juniata* were a serious-looking lot. With all the traffic on the Great Lakes, they had grave responsibilities. The three sisters operated for the Anchor Line until 1915 and then for the Great Lakes Transit Corporation, which took over many railroad vessels when Congress declared that the steamship subsidiaries must be divested to eliminate unfair competition. They sailed for the GLTC until 1936, and for three decades were considered among the most popular ships on the Lakes.

Right: The 168-foot (51.1m) *Owego*, built in 1853, was a typical early package freighter owned by the Erie Railroad. She, and sometimes as many as eleven other steamers, or "propellers" (as they were also known), sailed for the Erie's subsidiary, Union Steamboat, between the Dunkirk, New York, terminal and other Lakes ports, carrying mostly manufactured goods. Since there was virtually no tidal variation on the Lakes, vessels were built with side ports, or doors, through which cargo could be wheeled on ramps, avoiding the necessity of loading by derrick and winch. Other railroads had fleets as large or larger than Union's. For example, the Lehigh Valley Transit Company, established by the railroad in 1881, operated thirteen steamers (six wooden bulk freighters and seven steel package freighters), while the Delaware, Lackawanna & Western Railway operated eight, mostly package freighters. Nearly all the railroads with lines to the Lakes had a maritime subsidiary, some for as long as sixty years.

1915
"THE GREAT LAKES ROUTE"
ANCHOR LINE

OCTORARA
PENNSYLVANIA RAIL ROAD

The Erie & Western
Transportation Co.
J.C. EVANS   H.D. HOSMER
Vice-Pres. and Gen'l Manager   Gen'l Passenger Agent
ANCHOR LINE DOCK, BUFFALO, N.Y.

Panama Canal Act forced interstate railroads to divest themselves of their fleets. Most of the railroad-owned vessels (except for railroad-car ferries) were sold to the newly formed Great Lakes Transit Corporation, which continued to operate until its boats were taken over by the federal government during World War II.

Shipping on the lakes during the 1870s and 1880s underwent a technological revolution that paralleled railroad development. In the decade following the Civil War sailing vessels outnumbered steamers two to one, but both were still small and made of wood (156 tons [158.5t] average for sail and only 223 tons [226.6t] average for steam). By the late 1880s iron, then steel, hulls were becoming both practical and affordable (though still much more expensive than those constructed of wood), and vessels were getting larger and larger. So, by 1888 steamers outnumbered sailing vessels. The steamship, with coal-fired boilers and screw propulsion, was becoming faster, more powerful, and able to carry much larger cargoes. The typical Great Lakes bulk-carrier design, with engine and primary

THE ERIE AND WESTERN
TRANSPORTATION CO.
ANCHOR LINE
PENNSYLVANIA RAILROAD STEAMERS

Dinner

SOUP
Cream of Celery

FISH
Baked White, Wine Sauce

MEATS
Roast Beef Roast Lamb, Mint Sauce Boiled Ham

ENTREES
Apple Fritters Veal Croquettes

VEGETABLES
Mashed Potatoes Baked Potatoes
Boiled Onions Succotash Squash

FOWL
Roast Turkey

SALAD
Fruit

DESSERT
Rhubarb Pie English Plum Pudding Pumpkin Pie
Ice Cream Assorted Cake
Nuts and Raisins Fruit Edam and Dairy Cheese Water Crackers
Tea Coffee

STEAMSHIP JUNIATA Sunday, August 6, 1905

An additional charge of 25 cents each will be made for meals served in rooms

Right and below: The *Juniata*, sister to the *Octorara*, was built in 1905 (the third sister, *Tionesta*, came in 1903) and was the epitome of turn-of-the-century luxury. As can be seen in the attire of passengers in the dining salon, evening wear in those days did not include designer jeans. The menu, while not gourmet, contained sufficient courses to ensure that any passenger so disposed could participate in total gluttony. The three sisters were 360 feet (109.4m) long and had a cruising speed of 17 mph (27.2kph). Their regular route was between Buffalo and Duluth, with stops at all important ports in between.

deckhouse aft, began to be used in iron-ore carriers on the western lakes toward the end of the century. Many of the bulk carriers belonged to major steel producers. Package freighters and passenger vessels were on their way out, though they would not disappear completely until after World War II.

Chicago's success as a railroad-lake-river junction seemed unbounded, but the city itself could no longer contain the railroad traffic. Modest, then large, then enormous rail classification yards sprang up in the prairies around the city. Each railroad had its own yard (and in some cases two, three, or four), along with its own freight houses, roundhouses, offices, and auxiliaries. And they grew and grew. By 1937 the Chicago Terminal District, which extended all the way into Indiana, west to Joliet, and nearly seventy miles (112km) north to Waukegan, contained 160 freight yards, 275 freight stations, and more than seven thousand miles (11,200km) of track. More than six hundred freight trains a day groaned through the yards, pulling an average of seventeen thousand carloads to all points in the United States and many in Canada. The Illinois Central alone, in one year, moved more than seventy thousand carloads of coal, forty thousand carloads of grain, thirty-nine thousand carloads of automobiles, and nearly that number of refrigerator cars through the Chicago Terminal District.

Above: The *Mississippi*, built in 1853 for the Michigan Southern Railroad, was typical of early steamboats plying the Great Lakes (as well as Long Island Sound). Before steel strapping devices, huge timber hogging-arches were used to keep bow and stern sections, with little buoyancy, from sagging, or hogging. The *Mississippi* was 326 feet (99.1m) long, weighed 1,829 tons (1858.3t), had a walking-beam engine powering two paddle-wheels, and was of wood construction. For four years she ran between Buffalo and Sandusky, Ohio, but was laid up during the financial panic of 1857. By the time conditions improved, railroads connected the cities and, because she was expensive to operate, she was scrapped. For ten years beginning in the mid-1850s the Michigan Southern ran between six and eight luxurious steamboats between Buffalo, Toledo, Detroit, Sandusky, and other Great Lakes ports. All too soon they were made obsolete by the growth of the railroads and newer vessels.

Right: A Wheeling & Lake Erie Railroad engine pushes a hopper over the Cuyahoga River in the heart of Cleveland's industrial center in this scene from the late 1930s or early 1940s. Republic Steel's huge plant is in the background. The Wheeling & Lake Erie, in spite of its small territory—hardly more than five hundred miles (800km) of track—was generally healthy because it ran through the core of North America's heavy industry, carrying industrial components around northern Ohio and coal from Wheeling, West Virginia, and southern Ohio to the steel centers around Lake Erie. The Cuyahoga River divided the city in half, east from west.

But Chicago's success was also its failing. Even before the turn of the century the spaghetti bowl of tracks surrounding the city had become nightmarish, and shippers began to howl as their goods were delayed or, worse, lost as freight cars and sometimes entire trains were misplaced or overlooked in the godforsaken morass of Chicago's freight yards. More than a dozen belt-line and terminal-switching railroads developed for the sole purpose of transferring cars from one yard or industrial spur to another throughout the system. But no solution was perfect—or even good—and railroads began looking for ways to avoid the long delays in moving trains through Chicago.

Right: John Stockley's pier, built in 1849 from the end of Water Street, was the first pier at Cleveland. It extended 924 feet (280.9m) into Lake Erie. At center is the Ashtabula Railroad's "shop." The Cleveland, Painesville & Ashtabula Railroad was chartered in 1848, and by 1852, generally following Lake Erie's shoreline, reached Erie, Pennsylvania. The name was changed twice: after a merger in 1868, it became the Lakeshore Railway, and the next year, after another merger (with Michigan Southern), it became the Lakeshore & Michigan Southern. Cleveland's residents rejoiced at their good fortune in having both steamboat and railroad transport only fifty-three years after their fair city had been scratched from "the unbroken wilderness."

Above: Downtown Cleveland is shown in 1929 with the new Cleveland Terminal Tower skyscraper in the foreground. The low building just beyond and to the right is the Union Terminal Concourse, receiving New York Central, Baltimore & Ohio, Erie, New York, Chicago & St. Louis (Nickel Plate), and Shaker Rapid Transit passenger trains. The Pennsylvania Railroad had its own passenger station on East Fifty-fifth Street. Beyond the tower is "Collision Bend" in the Cuyahoga River, and next to it are the tracks of the Cleveland Terminal Railroad, which, using electrics, did all the passenger switching for the terminal.

Right: An experimental steam-powered coal dumper that never caught on. This elaborate and ponderous dumper probably loaded in a horizontal position. Upon having a special end-dumping gondola placed on it, perhaps by a donkey engine, the dumper pivoted on an axle hidden by the rotating machinery house. Then, once aligned, it tilted into the ship's hold. It is not clear whether the operator above the car controlled all movement or only the dumping. Once the car emptied, it probably rolled down to an empties yard while a loaded car took its place. This dumper, circa 1890 to 1900, was probably too slow. Also, it placed the operator in a somewhat unenviable position.

Below: A 1948 view of the Baltimore and Ohio's new coal dock at Lorain, Ohio. The electrically operated coal dumper takes loaded, seventy-ton (71.1t) coal cars up the ramp, flips them over to empty, and returns them to the "empties" yard. The coal, prior to being loaded in the vessel, is washed and sprayed with a solution to reduce coal dust.

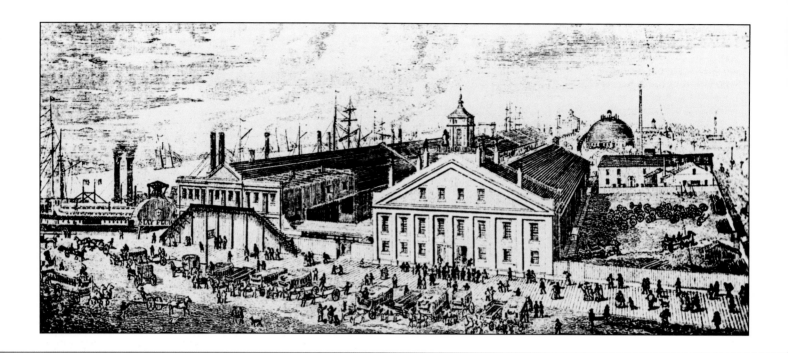

Top: The Michigan Central Railroad's Detroit Terminals and offices in 1850. The impressive building at right is the Michigan Central Depot, the first of two at the site, with the railroad's general offices above. To the left is the marine terminal, an enormous passenger and freight building along which can be seen the masts and stacks of various sailing vessels and steamers. Michigan Central's steamer *May Flower* departs at far left. The city's Cobol Hall, with its ice rink and the accompanying Renaissance Center hotel complex, was eventually built on this site, just north of the Ambassador Bridge and at the hub of Detroit's downtown.

Bottom: Huron was a small but thriving port in western Ohio in 1883. At left is the Huron Lumber Yard. The schooner *Mount Blank* unloads coal into Baltimore & Ohio gondolas. However, the Wheeling & Lake Erie is the only railroad with access to the port. In the distance is the breakwater protecting the harbor. Huron developed into a major coal and ore port and became the site of a large grain mill and elevator.

Right: An 1885 view of Michigan Central's Detroit facilities as seen from the opposite end of the marine terminal building (on right). The MC roundhouse is at center and its car-repair shop is just behind it and to the right.

Above: By the early 1900s Cleveland's industry and railroads were outgrowing the available area around the Cuyahoga River. A breakwater was built in front of the city, and behind it miles of docks and rail yards developed. This area, shown in about 1935, was on the eastern end of the breakwater. The new Cleveland Municipal Stadium is at far left, with downtown behind it. The New York Central's mainline and supporting tracks run behind the docks and stadium, from left to right, while the Pennsylvania Railroad's mainline runs from the rear, on the left bank of the Cuyahoga, a bit of which is shown at upper right with the excursion steamer Goodtime prominent. In the foreground, to the right of the stadium, are nine tracks of the New York Central and then fifty-eight tracks and three slips for large vessels all belonging to the Cleveland & Pittsburgh Railroad, a PRR subsidiary. Finally, on the far right, are twenty-five tracks and an abandoned (1932) nine-stall roundhouse owned by the New York Central.

Top right: A serene view of Lake Michigan in 1892. A Chicago & North Western passenger train arrives in Milwaukee from Chicago. Notice that while the buildings of most eastern cities were predominantly of stone, or brick, Milwaukee's were of wood, the northern forests still providing that material.

Bottom right: Bulk carriers are empty of cargo and laid up for winter at Jones Island, Port of Milwaukee, in 1938. On each side of the vessels are Chicago & North Western yards. The CNW developed extensive routes in northern Illinois, Iowa, Wisconsin, and Minnesota, and went as far south as Kansas City and St. Louis and as far west as Casper, Wyoming. Even though many of its routes duplicated those of the Milwaukee Road during the late 1800s and early 1900s, the CNW was a midwest railroad power.

Right: The *Monrovia* loads 6,300 tons (6,400.8t) of flour in 1959, then the largest amount loaded for an overseas destination from the Port of Milwaukee. Today this tonnage would be considered laughably small, and instead of loading thirty bags on a pallet in a sling, nearly all loading would be directly from elevators into bulk carriers and would require one-tenth the time and labor.

Below: Huletts unload iron ore from National Steel's bulk carrier the *Earnest T. Weir* at the Pennsylvania Railroad's West Breakwater Yard on the Cleveland lakefront in 1965. Each of the electric-powered Huletts moved independently of the others. All were mounted on rail-rolling frameworks that allowed them to slide toward or away from the vessel as well as move fore and aft. A Hulett arm extended over a vessel's hatch and a section of it dropped into the hold. An operator rode on the arm and controlled its movement as well as the bucket at its end. The bucket could pick up fifteen to eighteen tons (15.2–18.3t) of ore in one bite. The Hulett then reversed and deposited the ore in a rail car for transfer to a local steel mill or on to a stockpile for use during ice-bound months when lake vessels could not sail.

The Railroad Car Ferries

The spawning of railroad-car ferries was due not only to Chicago yard congestion but to other factors as well. Wisconsin and western Michigan port cities, particularly Milwaukee, a natural competitor with Chicago, saw them as a means of opening direct rail-water routes to other parts of the country, bypassing their rival. Also, ferries would eliminate the costly break-bulk loading and discharging from package freighters to railcars. Certain railroad owners, especially those who didn't have Chicago routes, thought that car ferries could boost revenues and give them an edge over their competitors. The Ann Arbor Railroad was a perfect example.

In 1892 the Ann Arbor's predecessor—the Toledo, Ann Arbor, and North Michigan, which for twenty years had been building a line northwest from Toledo via Ann Arbor—finally reached Elberta, near Frankfort, on Lake Michigan's eastern shore. Large sources of revenue had long beckoned seductively from across the lake, and the railroad was determined to make a Wisconsin connection. So in the same year that it completed its tracklaying, the line put into service the first railcar ferry to operate in open water on Lake Michigan. The 260-foot (79m) *Ann Arbor No. 1* was built with an oak hull steel-sheathed to four feet (1.2m) above the waterline. She had a four-track car deck, with a capacity of twenty-four cars, and an open stern for rapid loading (a design feature that left her susceptible to following seas sweeping through her car deck and into her boiler room). She and a sister, the *Ann Arbor No. 2*, were both designed for year-round icebreaking with reinforced plumb bows curved at the foot to ride up on and break ice, a bow propeller to aid in icebreaking, and twin individually controlled propellers aft for greater thrust and docking maneuverability. The Ann Arbor Railroad's car ferry operations were so successful that besides the original Kewaunee destination, it soon

Loading rail cars on the Mackinac Transportation Company's *Chief Wawatam* at Mackinac City, probably in the 1920s. The MTC was formed in 1881 by the Duluth, South Shore & Atlantic, the Michigan Central, and the Grand Rapids & Indiana to ferry merchandise and railroad cars across the Straits of Mackinac. Because of strong currents, bad weather, and great quantities of ice, a powerful vessel was needed. The *Chief Wawatam* (built in 1911, 338 feet [102.8m] long, and powered by three-triple expansion engines together producing 4,500hp) could carry twenty-six cars on four tracks and was an immediate success. She served for more than fifty years.

added two others (Manitowoc and Menominee) in Wisconsin and Manistique on the Upper Michigan Peninsula.

By the early 1900s the Ann Arbor ferries were hauling more than twenty-six thousand railcars a year, pushing freight revenues far higher than the road's directors could have dreamed possible. Nor were ferry-building costs unreasonable. The *No. 1* had cost only about $260,000 and the *No. 2* $280,000. Engine maintenance wasn't much more expensive than that of a railroad locomotive, and vessel maintenance cost far less than maintaining trackage to the same locations. In fact, with their 13-knot cruising speed, in good weather the ferries could make a round-trip to the Wisconsin ports in less than ten hours. The railroad's car ferry operations were vital to its existence, since they played a role in more than half of the road's freight movements. The Ann Arbor was one of the few railroads in the world to have greater ferry mileage (320 [512km]) than track mileage (292 [467.2km]).

The Ann Arbor's car-ferry triumph was not lost on other Great Lakes railroads. The Flint and *Pere Marquette*, a Michigan

Top right: The Wisconsin and Michigan Railway's Lake Michigan Car Ferry Transportation Company operated wooden car-ferry barges between South Chicago and Peshtigo Harbor on Green Bay beginning in 1895. Towing unwieldy 300-foot (92.2m) -long barges carrying up to twenty-eight rail cars nearly three hundred miles (480km) over open water on Lake Michigan was a risky proposition. Also, though car ferries could be operated in winter, the tug-barge combinations could not. The company folded after fifteen years.

Bottom right: In a famous photograph taken in 1896, the Ann Arbor Railroad's *Ann Arbor 1* sits trapped in windrow ice. The *Ann Arbor 1*, built in 1892 with a reinforced bow, two propellers aft for thrust, and a bow propeller for even more drive, was designed for operation in pack ice. Unfortunately, by the date of this photograph the bow propeller had been removed. The *Ann Arbor 1* served for eighteen years until she caught fire at Manitowoc in 1910. Her remains were rebuilt into a barge.

Right: The sleek *Arthur K. Atkinson* is shown here in 1959 shortly after she was rebuilt from the *Ann Arbor No. 6*, which had been constructed in 1917. The Atkinson was lengthened by thirty-four feet (10.3m), repowered with diesels and variable-pitch propellers, and totally made over topside so that it is impossible to tell that she had once been the *Ann Arbor No. 6*. Her alteration increased her capacity from twenty-six to thirty railcars.

Above: Milwaukee was still the rail-car ferry center of the United States in 1956, when this picture was taken. The Chesapeake & Ohio's car ferry the *City of Midland* (389 feet [118.3m], built in 1941) is at left, with automobiles in a shelter on her weather deck, while her sister, the *City of Flint 32* (369 feet [112.3m], built in 1930), departs and the *Ann Arbor No. 6* (338 feet [102.8m], built in 1917) is at right. The Ann Arbor Railway did not operate into Milwaukee with any frequency or on a regular schedule.

lumber railroad that was running out of trees, placed the *Pere Marquette*, the first steel-hulled car ferry, in service between Ludington, Michigan (originally named Pere Marquette), and Manitowoc, Wisconsin, in 1897. The *Pere Marquette*, hailed locally as a titan for her size and power, was 337 feet (102.4) long and had a capacity of thirty railcars and ten passengers in cabins on her main deck. Definitely a success, she ferried railcars for thirty-seven years.

In 1900 the Flint joined with two other Michigan lumber railroads to form the Pere Marquette Railroad (later Railway). By 1904, through acquisition of short lines and trackage rights, the Pere Marquette extended all the way to Buffalo along the north shore of Lake Erie, and south to Chicago, Detroit, and Toledo. While its extended operations required car ferries over the St. Clair River, the Niagara River, and the Detroit River and across Lake Erie, the Lake Michigan service

This photo of the Michigan Central/New York Central yard at Twenty-first Street, facing downtown Detroit, was probably taken in the 1930s. The yard was used for storing cars coming from or going to the Detroit-Windsor Railroad Tunnel, which had been built by the New York Central in 1910 and was used by it and its subsidiary, the MC, as well as by the major Canadian railroads. Both the Wabash and the Pere Marquette operated car ferries from the yard's perimeter. The vessel at right with three large stacks appears to be the Wabash ferry *Detroit*.

dwarfed them all. In fact, in terms of freight tonnage and the number of passengers and automobiles carried, as well as the number of vessels, the Pere Marquette and its successor, the Chesapeake and Ohio, ran by far the largest car-ferry operation on the Great Lakes. Carrying both coal and new automobiles, the railroad sailed between Ludington, Michigan, and Milwaukee, Manitowoc, and Kewaunee, Wisconsin. Passengers and their automobiles provided considerable income for the Pere Marquette. The railroad even planked over railroad car decks during the tourist season to increase this lucrative business. Even after World War II revenues remained high. In 1947 the Pere Marquette merged into the Chesapeake and Ohio (C&O), and in 1953 the parent railroad put into operation two modern car ferries, the 393-foot (119.5m) *Spartan* and *Badger*. Together with the 389-foot (118.3m) *City of Midland 41*, built in 1940, they were the largest on the lakes. Each could carry thirty-four railroad cars and had upward of sixty staterooms and the capacity for five hundred passengers. The C&O's postwar fleet consisted of seven car-ferries, which in 1961 carried 132,000 railroad cars, fifty-four thousand automobiles, and 153,000 passengers. In 1971 only three of the newest vessels remained, but still they carried nearly sixty-two thousand autos and 197,000 passengers. The Ann Arbor Railroad, the second largest on the lakes, that year carried twenty-nine thousand passengers and fewer than eleven thousand autos.

Unloading the *Pere Marquette 20* at Ludington, probably about 1930. The switcher is pushing an "idler," usually a flatcar, that often was used to keep the heavy weight of an engine off a float-bridge. In cases of extreme low tides on the coasts, it was used to keep the engine from high-centering at the bottom of the float-bridge.

The other large car-ferry service on Lake Michigan belonged to Canada's Grand Trunk Railway. It operated three 347-foot (105.5m) vessels—the *Grand Rapids* (1926), the *Madison* (1927), and the *City of Milwaukee* (1931)—between Milwaukee and Muskegon and Grand Haven, Michigan. A fourth vessel, the *Milwaukee*, foundered off its namesake city on October 22, 1929. The vessel's wireless had been removed by management to cut costs, but a scribbled note found later in a canister described the catastrophe: "The ship is taking water fast. We have turned around and headed for Milwaukee. Pumps are working but seagate is bent in and can't keep water out. Flicker is flooded. Seas are tremendous. Things look bad. Crew roll is about the same as on last payday." All fifty-two men onboard were lost.

Three other car-ferry services operated on Lake Michigan. The largest, the Lake Michigan Car Ferry Transportation Company, a subsidiary of the Wisconsin and Michigan Railroad, towed four enormous, unwieldy barges on two routes beginning in 1895. Their operation lasted about fifteen years— during which time three of the four barges sank, victims of storms and a collision.

Except for Lake Ontario's Ontario Car Ferry, Ltd., operated jointly by the Baltimore and Ohio and Grand Trunk Railway, the other significant operations were all on Lake Erie. The Lake Erie and Lake Ontario car-ferry lines all had a single purpose: to carry U.S. coal to southern Ontario. Nearly all the Lake Erie vessels sailed from Ashtabula and Conneaut, Pennsylvania, to a variety of Ontario ports. The exception was the Michigan and Ohio Car Ferry Company's carfloats, which operated between Sandusky and Detroit at the turn of the century.

The first railroad to operate car ferries on Lake Erie was the United States and Ontario Steam Navigation Co., a subsidiary of the predecessor of the Bessemer and Lake Erie Railway. In 1895 and 1896 its first two ships, the *Shenango No. 1* and *No. 2*, larger than but otherwise similar to the *Ann Arbor No. 1* and *No. 2*, went into service. The company also operated passenger steamers between Ontario ports and Cleveland.

Another Erie carrier, the Pere Marquette, along with a smaller road, the Bessemer and Lake Erie, for a time ran the Marquette and Bessemer Dock and Navigation Co. with an unenviable safety record: two of its four vessels were destroyed, one by fire, the other by foundering.

The Pennsylvania Railroad and Canadian Pacific jointly owned a subsidiary, the Pennsylvania and Ontario Transportation Co., which operated the thirty-car vessel *Ashtabula* from 1906 until she was destroyed by collision in 1958. The New York Central, not to be outdone by its main competitor, established the Toronto, Hamilton and Buffalo Navigation Co. in 1916 with the vessel *Maitland No. 1*, which lasted a mere sixteen years. Other small operations existed but often foundered along with their vessels. Eventually, the whole car-ferry system met that same fate.

When car ferries began to be used at the turn of the century, an average train might number twenty to twenty-five cars and easily could be carried on one vessel. By the 1920s both railcar size and train length had grown so much that as many as six car-ferry voyages consuming two or three days were required to transfer one train. Crew, fuel, and maintenance costs skyrocketed, especially with the outdated vessels still serving on most routes. By the early 1980s nearly all the car ferries were gone, along with most of the railroads that had operated them. In 1983 some Michigan businessmen bought the three C&O ferries for a dollar each in an unsuccessful attempt to keep the business afloat. The last vessel, the *Badger*, was refitted as an excursion ship in 1991 and still sails across Lake Michigan, but now she is loaded with vacationers instead of railroad cars.

PERE MARQUETTE

The two car ferries *Pere Marquette 21* and *22* were built by Manitowoc Shipbuilding in 1924. Both were originally 347 feet (105.5m) long, just under 3,000 gross tons (3,048t), and powered by two triple-expansion engines together producing 2,700hp, with room for thirty rail cars on four tracks. The ferries were lengthened in 1952 and 1953 by forty feet (12.2m) to accommodate thirty-two modern fifty-foot (15.2m) rail cars and were each repowered with two Skinner Uniflow compound engines, together producing 4,500hp. The

Pere Marquette 20, built in 1903 by Cleveland American shipbuilding, was nine feet (2.7m) shorter than her two younger sisters. Her engines together produced 2,280hp, and she also could carry thirty railcars. The *P.M. 20* was the last in a series of four, preceded by the *P.M. 17, 18*, and *19*, all built by American Ship Building in Cleveland. The *P.M. 17*, built in 1901, differed from the others in having fifty cabins and additional berths to serve 250 passengers. These boats were replaced by the *P.M. 21* and *22* and by the later *City of ...* vessels, all more powerful and ice-capable.

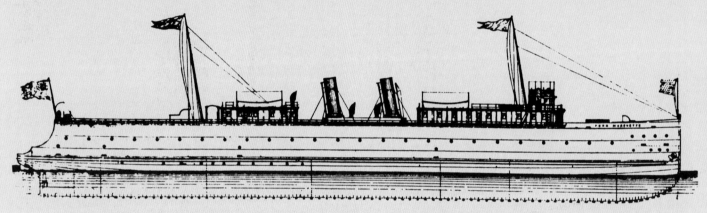

Above and right: A sketch and a cross-section of the *Pere Marquette 20*. Note the high ratio of machinery space to cargo (rail car) and quarters. Note also how little the exterior designs of these ferries had changed in twenty-one years.

Opposite: The *Pere Marquette 21* with her sea gate raised. The sea gate was developed in response to the sinking of car ferries due to following seas sweeping through their car decks, filling their engine rooms, putting out the fires in their boilers, and leaving the vessels to founder.

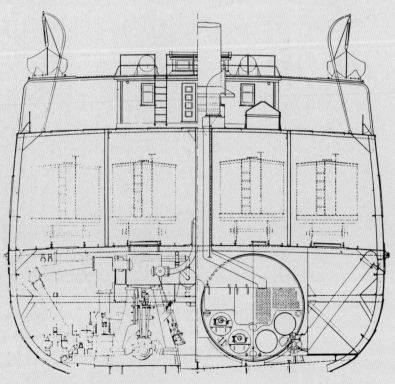

Left: For railroad car ferries, the *Pere Marquette*s had a good deal of grace, even with their plumb bows, which represented the end of an era in vessel design. In fact, the same design was followed in a total of six vessels: two *Pere Marquette*s, the *Ann Arbor No.7*, and three Grand Trunk Milwaukee car ferries.

CHAPTER THREE
THE SOUTH

The Southern Railway took control of the Mobile & Ohio in 1901. They jointly owned the Mobile Dock Company, its warehouses, and its lumber wharf, pictured here. Lumber had become an important commodity to the port, perhaps second only to cotton. Notice that in the early 1900s lumber was not bundled, but simply stacked more or less evenly, with stickers (cross pieces) used to help separate the boards and allow them to dry evenly on both sides, preventing warping. Because lumber was loaded loose, gondolas or boxcars, rather than flatcars, usually carried it. Eventually the Mobile Dock Company and its properties were taken over by the Alabama State Docks and its terminal railroad.

Railroads were established in the South by the time of the Civil War, but most of them were short lines, often running from the tidewater west to nearby agricultural centers. They neither connected with each other nor formed a substantial north-south network that would have helped further the Confederate cause. The Central of Georgia, then called the Central Rail Road and Banking Company of Georgia, did participate, however, in one of the most important Confederate troop movements of the war. The Central of Georgia transported General Longstreet's army from Virginia almost to Chickamauga (near Chattanooga, Tennessee), enabling the South to win the Battle of Chickamauga.

Subsequently, most of the Central of Georgia was destroyed in Sherman's march on Savannah in 1864.

Because the North controlled the Atlantic and because its blockade was so successful, the Union benefited from the southern ports nearly as much as the Confederacy did. During Grant's siege of Richmond in 1864, the U.S. Military Railroad took over the captured South Side Railroad, which ran inland from the deep-water port of City Point, Virginia, through Petersburg to Lynchburg. Unfortunately for the Union, many South Side engines and cars had been destroyed before the road's capture, and the remaining equipment could not handle the mountain of supplies arriving by sea. To remedy this situ-

The Union forces at City Point, Virginia, renamed the expanded terminal railroad the City Point and Army Line. It was operated by the U.S. Military Railroads, which had brought both engines and cars by barge from the north. Shown are the City Point enginehouse and three of its 4-4-0 locomotives. The *President*, built by Eastwick and Harrison, had been taken over from its former owner, the Winchester & Potomac Railroad. The locomotive and its backward-facing tender are pushing a line of cars loaded with fill to enlarge the embankment.

ation, the Military Railroad loaded twenty-four new locomotives and 275 new boxcars on a fleet of ninety carfloats at Baltimore and other northern ports and floated them down the Chesapeake and up the James River to Manchester, opposite Richmond, where they were unloaded at a newly completed railway wharf. Thus the Union, while cutting off Confederate supply lines from the west and south, was able to keep its own armies well supplied, a prime factor in the defeat of the Confederate Army of Virginia the following year at Richmond and Appomattox and in the South's subsequent capitulation.

Following the war, the rebuilding of ports and railroads proceeded slowly. Norfolk, Virginia, and Savannah, Georgia, became the two dominant ports in the southeast. In 1885 the Norfolk and Western, a major coal mover from the Appalachians, began shipping coal from Lambert Point, near

Top: To bring engines and cars south, the U.S. Military Railroads fastened together pairs of wooden Schuylkill coal barges, then placed long, heavy timbers on them to which eight tracks were secured. The carfloats could each carry eight freight cars or probably four engines and their tenders. Towed from Alexandria on the Potomac River (shown here) to City Point and, later, Manchester, this was the first military car-ferry operation in the world and was a great success.

Bottom: As Union forces captured more and more territory around Richmond, they developed new supply facilities closer to the just-established front lines. Here, in 1865, box-cars are being unloaded at Manchester, on the outskirts of Richmond on the James River.

Norfolk, and general merchandise to and from three ocean terminals in and around Norfolk. The Chesapeake and Ohio, a direct competitor, shipped from Newport News and for many years was the largest coal carrier in the South. The Norfolk and Southern ran from Norfolk south through the Tidewater to Morehead City and Beaufort, North Carolina, and west to

Charlotte. It used carfloats and lighters to cross the Elizabeth River to reach its northern terminus. It also had connections with the Old Dominion Steamship Company.

In the early 1880s a group of Southern railroads, including the Seaboard and Roanoke, the Richmond and Danville, the Chesapeake and Ohio, the Atlantic Coast Line and the Norfolk Southern, took control of the Old Dominion Steamship Company. The Old Dominion ran as many as eight passenger steamers from New York to connect with the railroad's various trains at Norfolk, Petersburg, and Richmond.

Right: A photo of the New York, Philadelphia & Norfolk's Port Norfolk Terminal on the Elizabeth River, near the mouth of Chesapeake Bay. These large four-track barges were between 300 and 350 feet (91.2–106.4m) long. Their pilothouses contained crew quarters and a steering station. The stacks projecting from the pilothouses were exhausts for boilers that powered a steering engine located in the hull. The large wheels on the floatbridges are winch handles used to tightly secure a barge to the floatbridge.

Above: The New York, Philadelphia & Norfolk Railroad's Port Norfolk Terminal was located in present-day Portsmouth, Virginia, and was the southern end of a thirty-six-mile (57.6km) crossing of Chesapeake Bay and the James River, opposite Cape Charles, Virginia. The 0-6-0 switcher is loading one of two four-track barges (the large-capacity vessels were designated "barges" rather than carfloats), designed to be towed on a hawser behind a large tug. The undated photo likely was taken before 1906.

It also operated steamers on feeder lines around Chesapeake Bay and the James River. Old Dominion was a success for nearly forty years, until railroad trunk lines' rapid service to New York caused its traffic to dwindle and eventually forced its sale in 1924. Eventually both the Norfolk Southern and the Norfolk and Western became part of the Southern Railway System. Norfolk was also served by the New York, Philadelphia, and Norfolk Railroad, a Pennsylvania Railroad subsidiary, which from 1866 to 1920 ran from southern Pennsylvania almost to Norfolk and used a number of steam-ers and carfloats as well as the side-wheel transfer steamer *Cape Charles* to cross Chesapeake Bay. The Chesapeake and Ohio RR also operated a small fleet of steamers and carfloats primarily from Norfolk to Newport News.

Norfolk's major competitor was Charleston, South Carolina, which, prior to the advent of the railroads, bustled as a shipper of rice and cotton to Europe and the northern states. Coincidentally Charleston was also a pioneering city with regard to railroading. In an effort to divert freight and passenger traffic from the other southern rival, Savannah, in 1830

Coal pier 5, on the right in the photograph on the next page, was a "low-level lake type" that was built just before this photograph was taken. It picked up hoppers, or gondolas, rotated them, and then dumped their loads into a pan-feeding conveyer. Here, coal is being loaded into a small collier. The operator of the dumper sits in the little house on the right, and the operator of the trimmer, which moved to evenly fill the ship's holds, sits in the house hanging over the water on the seaward side of the ship.

some Charleston businessmen built a rail line from Hainburg, on the Savannah River, to Charleston. This was all well and good, except that the municipal fathers, not quite as visionary as the railroaders, didn't want the messy thing in their fair city. So instead of puffing all the way to the harbor, the South Carolina and Canal Company's first engine, *The Best Friend of Charleston*, had to stop on the edge of town, where goods and passengers were unloaded and then taken by wagon to the docks. And so the advantage over Savannah was lost. Still, within three years Charleston's railroad, with 136 miles (217.6km) of track, became the world's longest.

Savannah triumphed in the end. Charleston's harbor was destroyed in the Civil War, and by the time it was restored, the city's two major railroads—the Southern Railway, which had taken over the South Carolina and Canal, and the Atlantic Coast Line—had established major interests in shipping to and through Savannah. Unfortunately for Charleston, the two railroads also controlled the Charleston Terminal Company, which

Right: By 1911, the date of this schedule, Old Dominion was an important coastal Atlantic carrier with six three-thousand-to-four-thousand-ton (3,048t–4,064t) passenger vessels with triple-expansion steam engines, such as the pictured S.S. *Madison* (353 feet [107.3m], 3,734 tons [3,793.7t], built by Newport News Shipbuilding in 1911). Besides her ocean fleet, Old Dominion was then running three two-hundred-foot (60.8m) bay and river steamers. In 1924 Old Dominion, no longer of interest to her railroad owners, was sold to Eastern Steamship Lines.

Right: The Norfolk & Western Railroad's enormous Lambert's Point coal piers on the Elizabeth River at Norfolk in 1936. In the foreground are the inbound coal-car receiving yards. On the far right only a small portion of the outbound-empty car yards is visible. Of the four coal piers, the two on the left are old-style high-level gravity-feed docks from which, originally, bottom-dump hoppers dropped coal into chutes directly alongside vessels being loaded. During World War I direct loading from hopper cars was replaced by electric-powered transfer cars that were loaded via dumper and run out onto the pier before they, in turn, were dumped. Both piers were retired as obsolete in 1937. Pier 4, second from right, was built as a high-level pier but designed to use rotary dumpers and electric transfer cars from the outset. The dumpers turned either hoppers or gondolas almost upside down, emptying them into the electric transfer cars.

Top: The *Yazoo*, a 210-foot (63.8m) wooden screw steamer, built in 1863 in Mystic, Connecticut, was one of Old Dominion Steamship's first passenger vessels on the Norfolk–New York run. She and five other auxiliary steamers came as part of the merger of the N.Y. & Virginia S.S. Co. and the Virginia Line (of the Atlantic Coast Mail S.S. Co.), which formed Old Dominion. By the time the railroads acquired the company in 1880, she and her sisters had been sold. However, she was representative of the early type of coastal vessel used by the railroads.

Center: By the time the steamer *Kansas City* (3,679 tons [3,737,9t], 327 feet [99.4m]) joined the Savannah Line's fleet in 1889, the company had upgraded its old wooden paddle-wheelers to nine newer iron screw-steamers, which ran on an average of twice a week to New York, Boston, and Philadelphia. The Savannah Line—or the Ocean Steamship Company of Savannah, as it was properly known—was not just an important subsidiary of the Central of Georgia Railway, it was absolutely critical for the railroad's survival in its competition against much larger southern rivals with better north-south connections.

Bottom: The Ocean Steamship Company's main Savannah terminal had been rebuilt in the early 1920s and over the following years was significantly expanded. By 1923, the company was running eight modern passenger steamers to New York and Boston, including the 381-foot (115.8m), 5,861-ton (5,954.8t) sister ships the *City of Birmingham* and the *City of Chattanooga*, both of which had been built by Newport News Shipbuilding.

owned nearly all the town's commercial waterfront. The two railroads prevented the port from developing until 1922, when the city finally bought all the Terminal Company's land. But it was too late. The port of Charleston never regained its early prominence.

Savannah's growth as a port city also resulted from her excellent waterborne connections with the Northeast. By the 1870s the Central of Georgia Railway (then still called the Central Rail Road and Banking Company of Georgia), along with its subsidiaries, controlled a rail network of more than seven hundred miles (1,120km) joining Savannah with Atlanta, Macon, Columbus, Albany, and Augusta. In 1872 the railroad took control of the Ocean Steamship Company of Savannah and its six side-paddle steamers. New vessels were built, and in 1881 the company acquired the Philadelphia and Southern Mail Line. Six years later it bought the Boston and Savannah S.S. Company. By the late 1880s the Savannah Line's nine screw steamers were sailing nearly every other day to New York, Boston, and Philadelphia. The Savannah Line continued until 1942, a remarkable seventy years, and in no small measure helped to develop Georgia.

Above: Even a very small railroad, like the South Carolina & Georgia, if it serviced a port city, often tried to create an advertising and scheduling tie-in with a steamship line that sailed to its largest off-track markets, as evidenced by this 1875 example announcing connections to New York and Boston. If the SC&GRR was not able to provide travelers from Asheville, Greenville, and Columbia with connections to the Northeast, rival Central of Georgia Railroad and its steamship subsidiary, the Savannah Line, would be most happy to oblige.

Above: Weighing cotton bales at the Central of Georgia's Savannah Cotton Terminal at the turn of the century. In 1904 it billed itself as the world's largest cotton terminal; yearly it handled more than 1,250,000 five-hundred-pound (226.5kg) bales, shipping them to the Northeast, to Britain, and to Europe. By 1913, however, Savannah had been overtaken as a cotton port by both New Orleans and Galveston.

THE COOL GREEN ROAD
TO VACATIONLAND

S O S C

SAVANNAH
· · · LINE · · ·

OCEAN STEAMSHIP CO. of SAVANNAH

NEW YORK · BOSTON · SAVANNAH

 NEW YORK — SAVANNAH — BOSTON

Fast Freight—South and West

Special attention is called to our excellent Package Car Schedule on freight from and via New York and Boston to all important points in the South, Southwest and West. Freight is loaded direct into cars alongside ship at Savannah, to break bulk at destination. No other transfer.

Below is shown the schedule time from New York; when from Boston add two days.

DESTINATION		BEST ROUTES		
		Atlantic Coast-Savannah Line	Central Savannah Line	Seaboard Savannah Line
Albany	Ga.	4 days	4 days	4 days
Americus	Ga.		4 days	4 days
Athens	Ga.		4 days	
Atlanta	Ga.		4 days	
Augusta	Ga.		4 days	4 days
Bainbridge	Ga.	4 days	4 days	
Birmingham	Ala.		5 days	
Cairo	Ill.		6 days	
Chattanooga	Tenn.		5 days	
Colorado Springs	Colo.		9 days	
Columbus	Ga.		4 days	4 days
Cordele	Ga.		4 days	
Cuthbert	Ga.		4 days	
Dawson	Ga.		4 days	
Denver	Colo.		9 days	4 days
Dublin	Ga.		4 days	
Enid	Okla.		8 days	
Eufaula	Ala.		4 days	5 days
Fernandina	Fla.			
Ft. Smith	Ark.		7 days	
Griffin	Ga.		4 days	4 days
Jacksonville	Fla.	4 days		4 days
Joplin	Mo.		7 days	
Kansas City	Mo.		7 days	
La Grange	Ga.		5 days	
Little Rock	Ark.		6 days	4 days
Macon	Ga.		4 days	
Memphis	Tenn.		5 days	
Meridian	Miss.		6 days	
Milledgeville	Ga.		4 days	
Millen	Ga.		4 days	
Mobile	Ala.		5 days	5 days
Montgomery	Ala.		5 days	
Nashville	Tenn.		4 days	
Newnan	Ga.		11 days	
Ogden	Utah		7 days	
Oklahoma City	Okla.		7 days	
Opelika	Ala.		4 days	
Paducah	Ky.		6 days	
Pensacola	Fla.		5 days	
Pueblo	Colo.		9 days	
Roanoke	Ala.		4 days	
Rome	Ga.		4 days	
St. Louis	Mo.		7 days	
Salt Lake City	Utah		11 days	
Sapulpa	Okla.		7 days	
Springfield	Mo.		6 days	
Statesboro	Ga.		4 days	
Talladega	Ala.			5 days
Tampa	Fla.	5 days	5 days	
Tallahassee	Fla.	4 days		
Thomasville	Ga.	4 days		
Tulsa	Okla.		7 days	
Union Springs	Ala.		4 days	
Valdosta	Ga.	4 days	4 days	
Waycross	Ga.		5 days	
West Point	Ga.		8 days	
Wichita	Kan.			
Vbor City	Fla.	5 days		

For further information apply to T. N. COOK, Freight Traffic Manager
New Pier 46, North River, New York, N. Y.

GENERAL OFFICES

Chas. H. Markham	Chairman of the Board, 138 East 11th Place	Chicago, Il.
A. E. Clift	President	Savannah, Ga.
E. R. Richardson	Vice-Pres. and Gen. Manager	New York, N. Y.
T. M. Cunningham	Vice-Pres. and General Counsel	Savannah, Ga.
H. T. Gill	Asst. to Vice-Pres. and Gen. Manager	New York, N. Y.
W. I. Percy	Superintendent	New York, N. Y.
T. N. Cook	Freight Traffic Manager	New York, N. Y.
J. S. Combs	General Freight Agent	New York, N. Y.
G. R. Angevine	General Passenger Agent	New York, N. Y.
A. R. Storey	Commissary	New York, N. Y.
W. Tanis	Port Steward	New York, N. Y.
W. B. McKinstry	Comptroller	Savannah, Ga.
M. F. Harden	Auditor	Savannah, Ga.
M. B. Nichols	Auditor of Disbursements	Savannah, Ga.
H. L. Fulton	Auditor of Traffic	Savannah, Ga.
C. F. Groves	Secretary	Savannah, Ga.
W. C. Askew	Treasurer	Savannah, Ga.

PASSENGER TRAFFIC REPRESENTATIVES

HAROLD A. ABRAMS, New England Passenger Agent,
Pier 42, Hoosac Tunnel Docks, Boston, Mass.
J. MERRICK EGAN, Traveling Passenger Agent,
New Pier 46, N. River, New York, N. Y.
A. P. McPETERS, Passenger and Ticket Agent, 37 Bull St., Savannah, Ga.
J. E. CARMACK, District Passenger Agent,
903-5 First National Bank Bldg., Atlanta, Ga.
R. W. RISER, General Southern Traffic Agent,
903-5 First National Bank Bldg., Atlanta, Ga.
W. H. CHISHOLM, European Traffic Manager,
Lloyd's Bldg., Leadenhall Street, London, E. C. 3, England

CITY TICKET OFFICES

BOSTON, MASS.	Pier 42, Hoosac Tunnel Docks
NEW YORK, N. Y.	{ 551 Fifth Avenue at 45th St. New Pier 46, North River
SAVANNAH, GA.	37 Bull Street

FREIGHT TRAFFIC REPRESENTATIVES

T. L. RYAN, Commercial Agent......New Pier 46, N. River, New York, N. Y.
F. L. VALDEZ, Trav. Commercial Agt. New Pier 46, N. River, New York, N. Y.
E. J. FINNEGAN, Freight Sol. Agt....New Pier 46, N. River, New York, N. Y.
W. C. DUNCAN, JR., Freight Sol. Agt. New Pier 46, N. River, New York, N. Y.
C. J. BROOKINGS, Commercial Agent,
Pier 42, Hoosac Tunnel Docks, Boston, Mass.
W. F. LIGHTBOURN, Commercial Agent,
Pier 42, Hoosac Tunnel Docks, Boston, Mass.
R. W. RISER, General Southern Traffic Agent,
903-5 First National Bank Bldg., Atlanta, Ga.
H. C. ERWIN, Commercial Agent. 903-5 First National Bank Bldg., Atlanta, Ga.
C. W. HART, Traveling Freight Agent,
903-5 First National Bank Bldg., Atlanta, Ga.
O. P. JONES, Freight Sol. Agent. 903-5 First National Bank Bldg., Atlanta, Ga.
E. W. WHITE, General Agent......912 Planters Bldg., St. Louis, Mo.
TINSLEY SMITH, Commercial Agent............Denham Bldg., Denver, Colo.
W. P. COLEMAN, Freight Service Agent.......Denham Bldg., Denver, Colo.
W. H. CHISHOLM, European Traffic Manager,
Lloyd's Bldg., Leadenhall Street, London, E. C. 3, England

PORT AGENTS

J. W. REILLY, Port Agent........New Pier 46, N. River, New York, N. Y.
L. WILDES, Port Agent......Pier 42, Hoosac Tunnel Docks, Boston, Mass.
H. M. EMERICK, General Agent..................Savannah, Ga.

TERMINALS

New York: New Pier 46, North River (just north of Christopher Street).
To reach New York Terminal use:
Elevated, surface or subway lines to 8th Street or Christopher Street, thence Crosstown line to North River.
Boston: Pier 42, Hoosac Tunnel Docks (City Square).
To reach Boston Terminal use:
Sullivan Square or Everett elevated train from North or South Stations or Boston proper to City Square, Charlestown.
Savannah: Ocean Steamship Company's Terminal.

22

Top: The Central of Georgia did not totally dominate traffic in and out of Savannah. The city had long been served by the Atlantic Coast Line, the Southern Railway, and the Seaboard Air Line. Seaboard had its own sizable ocean-freight terminal, shown here across the Savannah River from the city in the early 1920s.

Above, left and right: As the major trunk lines extended their routes, it became more and more difficult for the smaller roads, like the Central of Georgia, to compete. This situation was partially remedied in 1907, when E.H. Harriman, who controlled the Southern Pacific, Union Pacific, Illinois Central, as well as smaller roads, took over the Central of Georgia. This chart, from a 1930 Savannah Line schedule, is evidence that, with the help of the Illinois Central and its connections, the Central of Georgia could advertise—with at least some credibility—advantageous routes and connections to many cities.

Right: New 1935 Studebakers are shipped overseas. This photograph (taken at Norfolk & Western's Pier L, Lambert's Point, Norfolk) shows the "revolutionary" Pennsy auto-loading, double-door boxcars that allowed fairly rapid loading and unloading of the larger automobiles of the 1930s. There was no such thing as roll-on, roll-off loading of vessels then; each auto had to be individually loaded in a sling.

Below: McCullough's Docks, Norfolk, in 1895, was one of three Norfolk & Western general merchandise terminals in and around Norfolk. This view is from the present site of City Hall Avenue on the edge of downtown, facing the Elizabeth River.

⚜ Florida ⚜

Florida's railroad growth, and indeed her entire development, not only lagged behind the other coastal states but was split, east from west. Separated by a mass of lakes and swamps running down the center of the state, Atlantic Coast and Gulf Coast cities developed independently with few overland connections. Before the 1880s it took four days to travel on a quaggy wagon road the two hundred miles (320km) from Jacksonville to Tampa. Florida's railroads totaled only 485 miles (776km) in 1864, and by 1880 they had added only two miles (3.2km).

On the east coast, south of Jacksonville, not even a large town existed prior to 1890. On the Gulf, Pensacola had the greatest antebellum population—nearly three thousand— while Tampa's residents numbered only about five hundred.

One man put Florida on the map. Henry Flagler's hotel-railroad-shipping empire connected Florida to the world. Born in 1830 with business in his blood, Flagler was already by the age of twenty-two a successful grain-shipper in Ohio. There he first met John D. Rockefeller, then in the same trade. When Rockefeller turned to oil refining, Flagler joined him in this enterprise of the future. Together they built the Standard Oil Company, which by 1869 was one of the largest refiners in the country.

Flagler made his first trip to Florida during the winter of 1878, accompanying his sickly wife, who had been advised by her physician to winter in a warm climate. However, they trav-

A P&O S.S. Company brochure, obviously aimed at the winter tourist trade, reassures northeasterners accustomed to rough winter weather that, though they will be traveling in winter, the seas will be calm. Forget about the hurricane season. The vessel pictured is the *Evangeline*, 351 feet (106.7m), 3,789 tons (3,849.6t), and built in 1912.

eled no farther than Jacksonville, since, as Flagler dourly noted, neither transportation nor accommodation existed south of that resort town. Even getting to Jacksonville required some persistence. When Flagler returned in 1884 with his second wife (his first wife died in 1881), the couple managed to reach St. Augustine via a dilapidated short-line railway and an undersized paddle-wheeler. Flagler found St. Augustine breathtaking, a perfect place for a resort hotel catering to the wealthy of the Northeast. So in 1885 he purchased some land there and returned with an architect and a business assistant to lay out the Ponce de Leon, the first of Florida's grand resort hotels. Its opening in 1888 established the foundation of Flagler's new empire.

By 1890 Flagler had largely retired from Standard Oil. With a fortune in excess of $50 million, he had already bought a second hotel in St. Augustine, and built a third. He'd also purchased three short-line railways operating between that town and Jacksonville. As Flagler saw clearly, luxury hotels couldn't succeed in Florida unless equally luxurious and dependable transportation connected them with cities in the North. Having amalgamated his railway holdings into the Jacksonville, St. Augustine and Halifax River Railroad, Flagler extended his line a further fifty miles (80km) to Daytona, where he had bought and enlarged another hotel. The well-built new railroad provided the last link in a splendid rail network extending all the way to New York City.

The 1890s saw Flagler absorbed in enlarging his grand domain. All up and down Florida he was regarded as a hero, a savior to lead the state and its people to unheard-of wealth and progress. In 1894 he extended his railroad line to what would become West Palm Beach, bringing vacationers to new hotels he was building in Palm Beach, then extended it another seventy miles (112km) to Biscayne Bay, just across the Miami River from what in a few decades would be Florida's largest city. By 1896 his newly renamed Florida East Coast Railway ran 366 miles (585.6km) to Jacksonville.

If ever there was a father of a city, Flagler was Miami's. Not only did he pave the first streets in the sleepy village, build an electric plant, begin water and sewer systems, give land and financial assistance to establish four churches and a school, and construct the Royal Palm, a five-story resort hotel, he also dredged Biscayne Bay and built the deep-water port of Miami. And still he was not finished.

Henry Flagler's grandest scheme was to make Florida, and thus the United States, more accessible to Central and South America by means of a 128-mile (204.8km) -long railway to Key West, which would then become North America's most southerly port. The rail line would extend across the hundreds of Florida Keys and the ocean separating them. Compared to the major U.S. ports, Key West was hundreds of miles closer to the future Panama Canal (then under construction) as well as to Cuba, the new American "possession," and to all the ports and markets of Latin America and the Caribbean. Still, knowledgeable people thought Flagler was insane. One friend told him he needed a guardian. The engineering and construction hurdles

An early advertising piece for the East Coast Railroad promotes its founder, Henry Flagler; its over-water right-of-way, 126 miles (201.6km) to Key West, completed in 1912; Florida's agriculture; and its new status as a winter holiday spot. The Long Key Viaduct, shown here, featured more than two miles (3.2km) of concrete arches built over the Caribbean to Knights Key.

Above: A Florida East Coast express meets the Peninsular & Occidental steamer *General Cobb* at Key West, Florida, from which it will sail to Havana. In the 1920s, the Florida East Coast Railroad had more than 765 miles (1,224km) of track and ran 522 miles (835.2km) from Jacksonsville to Key West. The Cobb, built in 1906, was a 289-foot (87.9m), 2,522-ton (2,562.4t) steel vessel with three geared steam turbines, rated at 5,000hp.

were indeed formidable. In fact, no contractor would bid on the construction; so Flagler did it himself with his by now very experienced team of railway builders.

Construction was to take seven years. It began in 1905, and within a year the company had a workforce of as many as four thousand men and a fleet of eight stern-wheelers, twelve dredges, a dozen pile drivers, ten concrete mixers, eight derrick barges, 150 smaller barges, six locomotive cranes, and two oceangoing steamers.

Work progressed slowly. Concrete bridges and viaducts had to be poured, sometimes into watertight forms extending as much as thirty feet below the surface. Stretches of up to seven miles (12km) of open water had to be crossed. Not only was construction difficult, but five hurricanes impeded work and sometimes destroyed what had just been built. The worst hurricane, in 1906, carried away a floating workmen's camp and its occupants, more than seventy of whom were never heard from again.

Above: After opening a grand resort hotel in Nassau, Flagler's Peninsular & Occidental Steamship Company promoted the route heavily. The brochure reads, "The P&O S.S. Company operating a fleet of sea palaces bringing into close proximity the Anglo-Saxon and the Latin races, form a direct connecting link between the United States, Cuba and the Bahama Islands."

Right: The Florida East Coast in transition. An FEC F-7 hauls a string of highway trailers in the early 1960s. Intermodal operations were catching on around the country, and the FEC was not to be outdone, although the line's territory had shrunk considerably. In 1935 a hurricane had carried away forty miles (64km) of the Key West Extension, and the whole route to Key West had been abandoned. That, together with competition from larger railroads and from the trucking industry, kept the FEC from prospering.

Below: The Peninsular & Oriental Steamship Company docks in Miami in the early 1930s. These Florida East Coast Railroad cars are not meeting a vessel. They are being used as temporary housing for guests at a convention.

Other men were rescued by passing steamers. Even with all the impediments, however, the overseas extension was completed and opened on January 22, 1912, with a huge gala celebrated by trainloads of dignitaries and all of Key West's twenty thousand residents. The overseas railway would last for twenty-two years (twenty-one years longer than its builder). Henry Flagler believed that no storm could ever destroy his creation, but the Labor Day hurricane of 1935 washed away so much track and roadbed that the line had to be abandoned. Still, Flagler had been largely correct. None of the major bridges or viaducts were damaged. The state of Florida took over the right-of-way and on it built the overseas highway to Key West, which is still standing.

Besides the overseas railway, Flagler built a huge port at Key West through which he expected to ship goods and people on his own fleet to the major cities of Latin America.

Flagler already was in the steamship business. In 1898 he had bought a hotel and a small steamship company in Nassau in the Bahamas. His line carried freight, and especially passengers, to and from Miami, where they connected with his Florida East Coast Railway. Then he bought vessels to service routes from Savannah and Miami to Havana, Cuba, calling his new line the East Coast Steamship Company.

Meanwhile, Florida's Gulf Coast had undergone an even more spasmodic development. As early as 1850 many short lines had been chartered, but few laid any tracks, and those that did were destroyed during the Civil War. It wasn't until the late 1880s that the Louisville and Nashville Railroad—having taken over both the struggling Pensacola Railroad and the Pensacola and Atlantic—joined Florida's Gulf Coast to Mobile, Alabama, and to its main line running to Nashville, Louisville,

By 1896 the Louisville & Nashville had created a sizable general cargo facility at Pensacola—in fact, the largest in the South at the time. The warehouse at right is fifty feet (15.2m) wide by 1,202 feet (365.4m) long, has a capacity of five hundred carloads of freight, and contains three tracks on the first floor and two on the second fed by inclined trestles. The open-sided building was a most distinctive waterfront facility. The L&N also built a coal dock nearby. The photo dates from about 1910.

Memphis, and Cincinnati. The L&N developed Pensacola's port and went into the shipping business. Through its subsidiaries, the Export Coal Co., the Gulf Transit Co., and the Pensacola Trading Co., a small fleet formed to export Alabama coal and manufactured goods to Cuba, the West Indies, and Central and South America, returning with sugar, rice, and hardwoods. Pensacola Trading's two screw steamers eventually made regular trips to Liverpool and other English ports. In 1902 J.P. Morgan, who had taken control of the L&N, sold it to the Atlantic Coast Line, and the shipping business was eliminated. In 1925 Pensacola saw the arrival of the Frisco Lines, which linked it to the Midwest, but Pensacola as a port was small compared to Mobile, New Orleans, and Jacksonville.

Tampa, farther south than Pensacola, was even more isolated until Henry Plant, a wealthy transplant from Connecticut who had been buying Southern short-line railroads, came to its rescue. He purchased a partially built short line—the Jacksonville, Tampa, and Key West—and completed it to Jacksonville in 1884. Only then did Tampa have reliable connections with the rest of the state. In a few years Tampa's pre-railroad population of 720 had doubled and redoubled. By 1890 it had reached five thousand and by 1900, more than fifteen thousand. Tampa's port also developed as Plant extended his railroad, now called the Plant System, throughout the western

Above: The Pensacola & Perdido Railroad wharf outside Pensacola in the 1890s. The P&P was a short line operated by the area's largest lumber company. Sawn timber and raw logs were loaded, primarily on Scandinavian ships, for delivery to Britain, Germany, France, and Italy. To the right, above, is Fort Pickens, held by the North throughout the Civil War and never surrendered. A smooth-bore rifle used to defend the fort is at center. On the left is a scene from Palafox Street, a major Pensacola artery near the harbor.

Right: The U.S. 10th Cavalry (sans horses) boards U.S. government transport No. 23 (bearing a marked resemblance to La Grande Duchesse) at Port Tampa in 1898 on its way to Cuba. The Spanish-American War caused the mobilization of both railroads and shipping. Many commercial vessels were appropriated and trains chartered to move troops and supplies. The boxcars pictured here belonged to the Plant System, which would soon (in 1902) become part of the Atlantic Coast Line. Not long after, Plant's Savannah, Florida & Western was also acquired by the ACL.

part of Florida to join lines he already controlled in Georgia, Alabama, and South Carolina.

Plant also became involved in shipping. Starting with small steamers plying the St. Johns River south from Jacksonville, he bought oceangoing vessels to operate between Tampa and the Caribbean. By winter 1896 the Plant Steamship Line was operating two vessels weekly to Key West and Havana and one to Mobile, as well as its river sailings. In summer two vessels were shuttled to Boston, to run a twice-weekly vacationers' route to Halifax, Nova Scotia, and Charlottetown, Prince Edward Island.

Right: An early Peninsular & Occidental Steamship brochure cover advertising sailings to Cuba and Nassau, in the Bahamas. Advertising at the turn of the century obviously was not concerned with racial niceties. During this period Henry Flagler was busy expanding his shipping empire, taking on much of the Plant System fleet.

Below: A Louisville & Nashville 2-4-0 switches cars on the L&N Pensacola Wharf in 1916. Not only did the L&N develop the town's port, it created an international steamship company to sail from it. The L&N was already operating a line of small steamers to Havana and other Cuban ports and a line of steamers and coal barges to Galveston when, in 1894, it inaugurated steamship service to Liverpool. By 1895 it was running seven freighters carrying cotton, pig iron from Alabama and Tennessee, tobacco, and other commodities to England.

Henry Plant died in 1899. After his death his steamship company merged with Henry Flagler's East Coast Steamship Company to form one of the largest fleets in Florida. The Peninsula and Occidental Steamship Company became Florida's largest maritime transportation company, with sailings to the same destinations the two companies had previously serviced on their own.

Henry Flagler carried on alone after Plant died. He formed the Florida East Coast Car Ferry Company in order to operate three railroad-car ferries between his recently completed port of Key West and Havana. In May 1913, however, Flagler died, shortly before his new company was to start operations. Thus Flagler never saw the last piece of his transportation conglomerate become a reality.

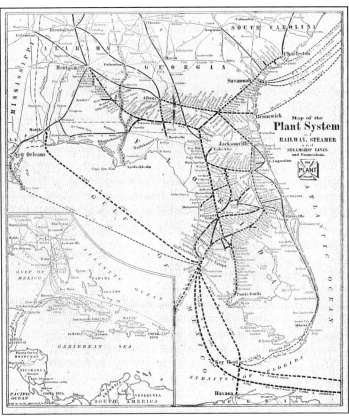

Above: By the time of Henry Plant's death in 1899, his vessels were sailing to Mexican Gulf ports and to Honduras, Jamaica, Havana, Santiago de Cuba, and Puerto Rico, as well as to New Orleans and Mobile. Add the Canada Atlantic and Plant Steamship Company sailings from Boston to Canada's Halifax, Charlottetown, and Hawkesbury, then top them with the Plant Railroad operations throughout much of the South, along with hotels in major Florida ports, and you have an amazingly large "system" developed by one man in a very short time.

Left: The Plant System railroads became a part of the Atlantic Coast Line Railroad in 1902. This gave the ACL access to Georgia and to most of central and southwestern Florida, including Port Tampa. The deepwater docks along Tampa's Hendry and Knight Channel are shown here in 1906 along with Atlantic Coast Line rolling stock.

Above: The Plant System, as its founder preferred to call it, expanded rapidly with four small vessels operating on the St. Johns River and the Manatee River and between local coastal ports not served by the railroad. A larger vessel, the *Florida* (230 feet [69.9m], 1,308 tons [1,328.9t]), joined the deep-sea fleet in 1887, serving more international destinations. Meanwhile, Henry Plant was establishing more hotels at his principal ports and his railroad covered most of northern Florida and had been extended to Montgomery, Alabama, in the west, and to Savannah and Charleston in the east.

Top right: *La Grande Duchesse* was to be the pride of Plant's fleet. Built in 1896 by Newport News Shipbuilding, she was 380 feet (115.5m) and 5,017 tons (5,097.3t) and had a 6,500hp quadruple-expansion engine. Unfortunately, the bossing-out of her stern limited her propulsion efficiency, and instead of a top speed of 18 or 20 knots, her best was only 13.5 knots. Also because of continual problems with her boilers, she served almost no time with the Plant fleet. After repairs she was chartered to the U.S. government to carry troops during the Spanish-American War, then was sold to the Savannah Line and renamed the *City of Savannah*. She met her end in World War I, sunk by a German submarine off the coast of New Jersey.

Right: In 1886 the Plant Steamship Line began semi-weekly service from Port Tampa to Key West and Havana, Cuba, with the new vessel *Mascotte* (pictured). She had just been built (1885) in New Haven, Connecticut, and was a 195-foot (59.3m)-long iron screw steamer of 884 tons (898.1t), with a 1250hp triple-expansion engine. She was joined the following year by a larger sister, the *Olivette*, 274 feet (83.3m) and 1,676 tons (1,702.8t). The brochure dates from 1890 or thereafter—service to Jamaica did not start until that time and the huge new Tampa Bay Hotel that Henry Plant built was not completed until 1890.

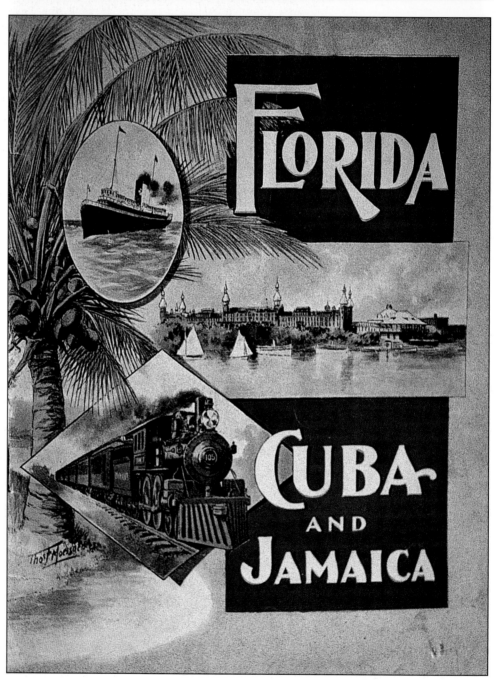

Right: The Florida East Coast Car Ferry Company was formed by Flagler just before his death in 1913 to transport rail cars from the end of his rail line at Key West to Havana, Cuba. The *Henry M. Flagler*, pictured, and a sister ship, the *Joseph R. Parrott*, were built by Wm. Cramp and Sons in Philadelphia in 1914. The vessels, 359 feet (109.1m) long and 2,699 deadweight tons (2,742.2t), were laid up after the hurricane of 1935 destroyed the rail line to Key West.

Above: Miami, the city that Henry Flagler raised from infancy. Flagler's railroad, running south 366 miles from Jacksonville and St. Augustine, reached the village of Miami in 1896. He dredged Biscayne Bay to create a deepwater port. Amalgamating his small railroads, he gave them the name Florida East Coast Railroad and almost single-handedly developed the city of Miami. This 1930s photo shows the fruits of his labors, with the Florida East Coast station in the foreground and the Dade County Courthouse at center.

The Gulf States

One of the first railroads to operate in the United States was not in sophisticated Boston or New York, where one might expect, but rather in rough-and-tumble Louisiana. In 1832 a small private road began steam operations along a five-mile (8km) line between New Orleans and Lake Ponchatrain to provide a connection with the lake's shallow-draft coastal vessels. The Ponchatrain Railroad became the first railroad west of the Appalachians. Twenty years later (in 1851) neighboring Texas got its first railroad, the Buffalo, Bayou, Brazos, and Colorado Railway, which by 1856 reached from Houston west to the Brazos River. But it was Galveston, not Houston, that for the next fifty years would be the transportation hub of the state.

Galveston, on an island fifty miles (80km) south of Houston, was first controlled for a short time by the pirate Jean Lafitte around 1800. After Monsieur Laffite's demise, however, the city grew quickly. By the time Texas became a republic in 1836, Galveston was already the major shipping point on the Gulf west

Top right: Morgan's Louisiana & Texas Railroad & Steamship Company terminal at Algiers, across the Mississippi from New Orleans, probably in the late 1870s before the river was accessible to deepwater vessels. Ferries brought both railroad and steamship goods and passengers across the river until 1883, when car-ferry service commenced.

Bottom right: The Southern Pacific carfloat *Mastodon* crosses the Mississippi at Avondale, about 1910, in this painting by A. Alaux. Built in 1909, the steel *Mastodon* could carry twenty-seven freight cars. At the time, it was the largest carfloat in the world. She and the *Avondale*, a wooden float with a twenty-one-car capacity, shared responsibility for carrying both passenger and freight trains between New Orleans and lines west. Smaller floats and car ferries had previously been used at Avondale and Algiers.

of New Orleans. After the Civil War the Galveston, Houston, and Henderson Railway linked the town with Houston. Then the Galveston, Harrisburg, and San Antonio Railroad also joined it to San Antonio, to the north. And in 1881 the Gulf, Colorado, and Santa Fe, to be known as the Gulf Lines, reached Fort Worth and was heading north and west. In 1887 it met tracks being laid by the Atchison, Topeka, and Santa Fe coming from Kansas City. Thus, by 1890 Galveston was connected to nearly all the population and agricultural centers in the state.

Building railroads in Texas to join ports with the cotton-growing areas to the north and west was a simple, straightforward proposition. Not so in Louisiana. The New Orleans, Opelousas, and Great Western Railroad was intended to fulfill the New Orleans dream of a rail line connecting that fair city to the cattle and cotton fields of Texas and perhaps to the Pacific Coast. Building it, however, turned out to be a construction nightmare. The road started at Algiers, just across the Mississippi from New Orleans, and ran west only a few miles before reaching the swamps, where the difficulties began. The builders first had to cross the Trembling Prairie, a vast bog, then in succession Devil's Swamp, Chacahoula Swamp, and Tiger Swamp. To lay track across the Trembling Prairie—a little crust of dirt floating on a lake—the laborers had to fill the shallows and drive pilings in deeper water to support trestles. The

A Galveston Wharf Company 0-6-0, built by American Locomotive Company in 1907, switches cars in front of one of the company's two grain elevators in the late 1930s. The company's eight 0-6-0 switches (all built by ALCO) ran over fifty-one miles (81.6km) of track, which had a capacity for 1,100, cars and did all the switching for the port. Southern Pacific's terminal facility adjacent to the port was serviced by that company's engines.

swamps were no better. The men often toiled submerged to their waists, bedeviled all the while by anopheline (malaria-carrying) mosquitoes, snakes, and alligators; not surprisingly, malaria and yellow fever decimated the workforce. Rail builders considered this swamp construction the toughest in the continental United States. And no sooner had the workers conquered the swamps than they reached Bayou Lafourche, where the river

steamers had to be given access; to accommodate the steamers, the engineers constructed a mule-operated drawbridge.

Trouble from a very different quarter hit just before the line's scheduled opening in March 1853. The first engine, a new Baldwin 4-4-0 named *Opelousas*, sank near Key West with the vessel that was carrying her. The builders must have been muttering, "Somebody up there doesn't like us." Fortunately,

once the beleaguered New Orleans, Opelousas, and Great Western finally opened, business was good. At its western terminus, Bayou Boeuf and later Brashear City (now Morgan City), it met steamboats bringing cattle from Galveston and other Texas ports. The railroad connection saved having to steam to New Orleans via the winding Mississippi Delta, then silted, undredged, and with many dangerous snags.

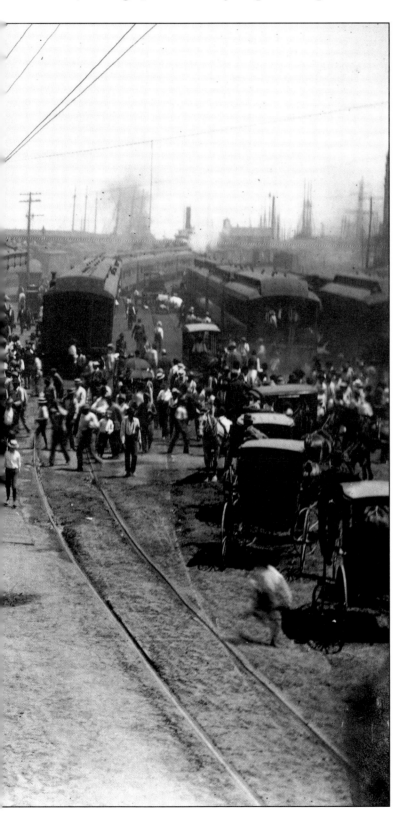

Steamships had been operating in the Gulf since Robert Fulton's *New Orleans* reached that city in 1812. Mostly these ships were small, shallow-draft paddle-wheelers that sailed principally between Texas and Mexican ports. A little later two of the major lines were owned by Cornelius Vanderbilt and by another shipping man, Charles Morgan.

Morgan had opened regular steamship service into Galveston in 1837 with his steam packet *Columbia*, and in 1858 or 1859 he purchased two of Vanderbilt's small steamers and added them to his fleet. Soon, however, the Civil War interrupted Morgan's plans for expansion.

As mentioned earlier, when the Civil War started, the South's railroads and manufacturing facilities were undeveloped compared to their counterparts in the North. Suddenly cut off from northern goods, the Confederacy was forced to create or find local substitutes, which could not be done on any large scale; so it tried to supplement its own production with European imports. The North countered with a blockade of all the South's ports. This led to the advent of the blockade runners, which began operating in late 1861.

In the 1860s Texas was still isolated from the rest of the South. Only three Gulf ports provided access to the interior by river and/or railroad: New Orleans, Pensacola, and Mobile. Naturally, the Union navy gave these their attention first. In May 1862 Commodore Farragut's squadron captured New Orleans. A month later Pensacola also fell. That left Mobile as the only port through which both the vast war machine and civilian needs could be supplied with goods delivered by the blockade runners. Lincoln and his chief planner, General Winfield Scott, hoped to starve the South into submission rather than attack it, but this they could not do without first controlling the Mississippi, and the South stubbornly held the river between Vicksburg, Mississippi, and Port Hudson, Louisiana.

Mobile then became the critical supply center for nearly half the Confederacy. Just as vital was Mobile's role transporting troops and equipment. In 1861 the Mobile and Ohio Railroad (M&O) had opened a line between Mobile and Columbus, Kentucky. This linked up with the east-west railroads that ran to Vicksburg on the Mississippi. In 1861 the Mobile and Great Northern Railroad (M&GN) began opera-

By the 1870s the Louisville & Nashville Railroad was also an important railroad presence in Mobile, providing transportation to both Montgomery and New Orleans. The city would soon have excellent connections with all of the South and Midwest as the L&N, the Illinois Central, and the Mobile & Ohio/Southern Railway developed extensive routes through both areas.

By the turn of the century the Mobile & Ohio docks had grown considerably, as shown here. Warehouses had been built, Mobile's first grain
elevator had been purchased, and trade was booming, with cotton and
other agricultural commodities being shipped to eastern cities and
even to Europe. The vessels pictured, mostly owned by European companies, were carrying lumber and cotton to Southern Europe.

tions, joining the just-completed Alabama and Florida
Railroad running between Montgomery and Pensacola. Thus,
by 1862 the M&O and M&GN systems made Mobile the only
link between Confederate armies in the east and west.

Although the east–west rail connection necessitated a
long southern detour and detraining at Mobile Bay for a
three-hour steamer voyage to the opposite shore, the system
went into service immediately upon completion. In 1862 twenty-five thousand men of the Army of the Mississippi were carried by train and steamer from Tupelo, Mississippi, to
Chattanooga, Tennessee, via Mobile. This was the largest single Confederate troop movement by rail during the war.
Others followed. Three thousand more troops were shipped
from Tupelo to Chattanooga to help defend the city. Their
timely arrival not only saved the city but allowed the
Confederate campaign to expand into Kentucky. Later, in

1862, a nine-thousand-man division came from Tennessee to
aid Vicksburg. Mobile also played a role in the last troop
movement of the southern Confederacy when in 1865 the
remnants of the Army of Tennessee straggled from northern
Mississippi to Montgomery, Alabama.

Mobile was the last major southern seaport to fall to the
Union before the Confederate States surrendered in 1865.

In 1866 the Federal government returned the sorry
remains of the South's railroads to their owners. The Gulf,
Mobile, and Ohio was slowly brought back to operating condition. The Louisville and Nashville, also newly revived, bought a
number of smaller roads and by 1888 connected Mobile and
Pensacola to its namesakes with lines extending as far north as
Cincinnati. Spotting this success, J.P. Morgan gobbled up the
Louisville and Nashville and then almost immediately sold it to
the Atlantic Coast Line.

But it was the New Orleans, Opelousas, and Great
Western—whose fate seemed so troubled from the beginning—
that probably suffered the most damage due to the Civil War.
Some of its engines had been shipped north and were never
returned; the rest were in terrible condition. Only forty-five

damaged freight and passenger cars remained of the 230 in service before the war. Bridges and rights-of-way were destroyed, and even the railroad's side-wheeler *Ceres*, used to transport freight across the Mississippi, had been blown up. The road struggled to rebuild, but in the shattered financial climate following the war, it went bankrupt.

Charles Morgan, the Gulf shipping magnate whose operations had been interrupted by the Civil War, picked up the devastated New Orleans, Opelousas, and Great Western at a sheriff's auction. He considered the risk worthwhile because the railroad's terminus at Morgan City still provided the fastest means of bringing goods and people north from the Gulf. He renamed the line Morgan's Louisiana and Texas Railroad. He also contin-

ued to enlarge his fleet, adding bigger and more capable screw steamers. By 1869 he was running four paddle-wheelers on the Mississippi as well as in the Gulf, and seven years later the Morgan Line had weekly scheduled sailings to New York and to Cuba, operating eight screw steamers from the Gulf ports.

In 1879 James Eads installed a system of jetties on the Mississippi Delta that reopened the silt-blocked passes, allowing large vessels to sail all the way to New Orleans. This innovation created immense opportunities for all the steamship operators, but since Morgan died the year the work was completed, he couldn't take advantage of them. At that time his shipping operation was second only to the Mallory Line in the Gulf, and his railroad began to expand into Texas.

Unloading mahogany logs at the Mobile & Ohio Railroad docks in Mobile, probably in the late 1880s. The M&O originated to help Mobile develop as a port by providing railroad connections to the Mississippi and Ohio rivers at Cairo, Illinois. The line was completed just in time for it to be destroyed in the Civil War. By the 1890s, however, it was a major factor in Mobile's growth, and the M&O had even started a small steamship line to Central America. Small schooners were common until the 1930s.

SEATRAIN

The largest and most deep-sea-capable railroad-car carriers ever used in the United States were the Seatrain vessels. Seven were built, and all had sixteen tracks running fore and aft, four on each of four levels. They carried a maximum of twenty-six cars on each of the two lower decks, thirty cars on the main deck, and nineteen topside on the weather deck. Loading was by means of the forerunner to the container crane and could be accomplished in about twenty-four hours. The Seatrains carried rail cars to and from Europe, along the Eastern seaboard in all seasons, to two Gulf ports, and to Havana, Cuba.

The Seatrain concept was established as a faster and cheaper means of transporting rail cars and their contents to Cuba and between the southern states and the northeast. The corporation was owned, in part, by the Texas Pacific and Missouri Pacific railroads. The first vessel, named *Seatrain* and later renamed *Seatrain New Orleans*

Left: The *Seatrain New York* was one of the first pair of vessels to be built by Sun Shipbuilding in Chester, Pennsylvania, in 1932. Note the loading well amidships and the enormous unobstructed weather deck.

Below: A typical Seatrain layout. Four removable loading cradles, complete with track segments, were part of each of the four decks (sixteen cradles in all). Cradle size was graduated, with the smallest at the bottom so each would fit through the deck openings above it. Rail cars were loaded on the cradles, and once in place on board, they were pulled fore or aft by cables led from winches. When a track on a given deck was filled, the last car was left on the cradle, which would be secured in place.

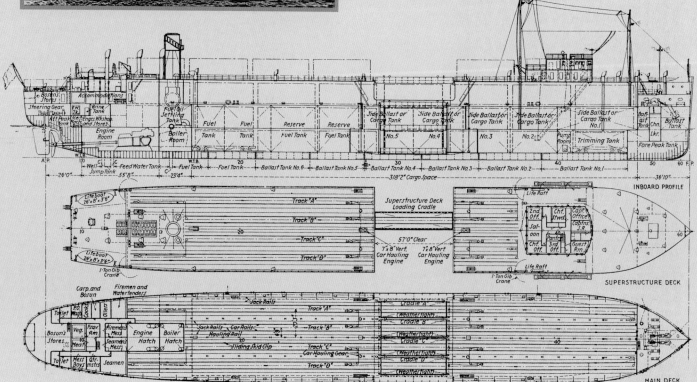

Inboard profile and plans of the superstructure and main deck

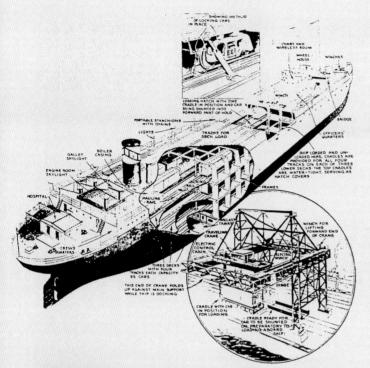

(all the vessel names were prefixed *Seatrain* followed by a city or state name), was built by Swan Hunter in Newcastle, England, in 1928. It measured 468 feet (142.3m) by sixty-three feet (19.2m) with a thirty-eight (11.6m) -foot draft and was 7,684 gross tons (7,806.9t). It was powered by a triple-expansion steam engine fired by two Scotch boilers and ran at 15 knots. Delivered in 1929, the *Seatrain* first ran between New Orleans and Havana. Three years later two more vessels, the Seatrains *New York* and *Havana*, were delivered. These and four more

Left: This cross-section shows how rail cars were loaded and secured. To fix a car in place rail clamps were first set against the trucks' outer wheels and tightened. Then jacks on threaded steel screws were set between jacking rails that ran outside every pair of car rails and car corners and turned until part of the car's weight was removed from the trucks. This system was essentially the same as that used on most of the Great Lakes car ferries.

Below: A freight car is lifted in its cradle. Loading time was eventually reduced to a car loaded every four minutes, an amazing speed considering the difficulties involved.

Seatrains—the *Texas* and the *New Jersey*, built in 1940, and the *Georgia* and *Louisiana*, built in 1951—were all fabricated by Sun Shipbuilding of Chester, Pennsylvania. All but the original ship were powered by steam turbines.

Prewar service was expanded from a port at Hoboken, New Jersey, to Havana and to Texas City, Texas. During World War II, the U.S. Army took over the ships. While it did use them to ferry rail cars and locomotives to provide some rail service for devastated coastal areas in the retaking of Europe, their principal cargoes were artillery, tanks, and aircraft. With their enormous open-weather and main decks, they were superlative transporters of heavy, unwieldy, and over-sized tools of war.

In 1947 Seatrain resumed service, adding a New York–to–Savannah run. In 1953 the Havana run was dropped, making Seatrain solely a coastal carrier competing directly with the major north-south trunk lines. The Central of Georgia, Monon, Grand Trunk, New Haven, and other regional railroads that had no extensive north-south routing supported and affiliated with Seatrain. The Southern, Seaboard, Atlantic Coast Line, and other southern carriers with routes to New York were bitterly opposed and fought Seatrain in lengthy Interstate Commerce Commission rate hearings. Eventually the small supporting railroads were taken over by larger, unsympathetic lines, and opposition to Seatrain mounted. Also, the new larger boxcars and auto racks (auto carriers) would not fit on the lower decks, and the vessels, as rail-car carriers, headed toward obsolescence. By 1967 the Seatrains had been converted to container ships, and in 1979 the line filed for bankruptcy.

This wonderful photograph shows a dozen boxcars locked in place, looking like models in a storage case. The scene is likely aboard the *Seatrain Louisiana* in 1951 at the Edgewater, New Jersey, terminal.

Before the Civil War, Texas had been effectively cut off from the rest of the country. To get there one had to travel either by boat or by hoof. After the war railroad construction became the state pastime. By the 1880s the Gulf, Colorado and Santa Fe (no relation to the older Santa Fe line) expanded further, connecting Galveston with Fort Worth, Houston, and East Texas. Then it came under the control of the other Santa Fe. Meanwhile the Katy (Missouri-Kansas-Texas Railroad) was building south from Kansas through Indian Territory (what would become Oklahoma), and the Southern Pacific (SP) was rapidly building across West Texas, working inward from El Paso on the west and San Antonio on the east. In 1883 the SP completed the first southern transcontinental railroad with through-train service from New Orleans to Los Angeles. Trains were loaded on

Top right: The *El Sol* (390 feet [118.6m], 4,523 tons [4,595.4t]) was a triple-expansion-engined steamer that had been built for Southern Pacific by Wm. Cramp & Sons in Philadelphia in 1890. She and a dozen other steamers shared the New York–Gulf Coast run for SP's Morgan's Steamship Lines.

Bottom right: The *Momus* (6,876 gross tons [6,986t], 10,770 deadweight tons [10,942.3t], built in 1906) was a combination passenger and freight steamer that, along with her sister ship the *Antilles* (built in 1907), had updated the SP New Orleans to New York fleet, now called the Atlantic Steamship Lines. Besides these vessels a slightly smaller sister, the *Creole*, was also built by Wm. Cramp & Sons in Philadelphia in 1907 for the same run. Four new fast (15 1/2 knot) freighters joined the fleet in 1910, sailing between Galveston, New Orleans, and New York. Two years later a tanker was built to supply oil from Mexico to the fleet, the world's largest railroad-owned fleet, with between twenty-five and thirty vessels, depending on the date.

carfloats at Algiers, on the west bank of the Mississippi, to cross to New Orleans. The ferry operation was eventually replaced by a bridge in the 1930s.

The New Orleans–Los Angeles line was promoted by the Southern Pacific as the "Sunset Route." It handled extensive passenger traffic and eventually became the most heavily used single-track freight route in the world. It was also the means by which its crafty president, Collis Huntington, managed to keep the entire transcontinental traffic to himself instead of sharing it with the Union Pacific and other roads.

As part of his empire-building, Huntington acquired the Galveston, Harrisburg, and San Antonio Railroad in 1874. Then in 1885 he took the big leap and bought Charles Morgan's entire holdings, both railroads and steamships. The Morgan Lines gave Southern Pacific a complete coast-to-coast transportation system under one management. In fact, with its Occidental and Oriental and Pacific Mail Steamship companies operating to ports in the Far East and its San Francisco and Portland Steamship Company operating on the California coast, Southern Pacific could carry cargo and people from Japan, China, Mexico, Central America, or Western Canada to New York solely on its own ships and trains.

Above: This Southern Pacific Atlantic Steamship Lines brochure (circa 1912) suggests both speed and luxury. The advertising boasts that "sea-going appetites are appeased in palatial dining rooms, where service is excellent and foods the best the market affords. Sitting rooms and bedrooms provide a complete relaxation to the traveler during 'One Hundred Golden Hours at Sea.'"

Right: A fine turn-of-the-century freighter loads cotton and bagged rice on the levee in New Orleans about 1905. With dredging and clearing of the channel to New Orleans, the city had become an important deepwater port and shipper of the South's agricultural commodities.

As a result Southern Pacific became the first major transportation conglomerate in the world, or at least in the New World. In 1900 the railroad's combined rail lines and Gulf steamship routes totaled more than 13,880 miles (22,208km). Adding Pacific steamship routes would probably have pushed the total to more than thirty thousand miles (48,000km).

By 1921 Southern Pacific's Morgan Line, then more commonly known as the Atlantic Steamship Lines, consisted of seventeen freighters, five passenger liners, and two tankers, along with a sizable fleet of tugs and lighters. The Atlantic Steamship liners, considered very luxurious for coastal trade, sailed three times a week from New Orleans with passengers and some cargo for New York. This New York connection extended Southern Pacific's fabled Sunset Route (to California), which lasted for more than half a century, until it was discontinued during World War II. Meanwhile, shipping operations had moved from Algiers to New Orleans after the further widening and deepening of the Mississippi Delta channels. So although New Orleans became the

Atlantic Lines' primary passenger center, Galveston remained the principal cargo port. Southern Pacific built a huge new cargo terminal there. With the terminal's modern electric conveyors and handling equipment and with the Atlantic's sixteen-knot steamers, SP boasted that cargo could move from Los Angeles to New York via Galveston in nine days, cutting six days off all-rail shipment times across the continent.

But Southern Pacific certainly did not have a lock on the Gulf ports. New Orleans was also served by the Louisville and Nashville, with lines to Alabama, Georgia, and Florida. The

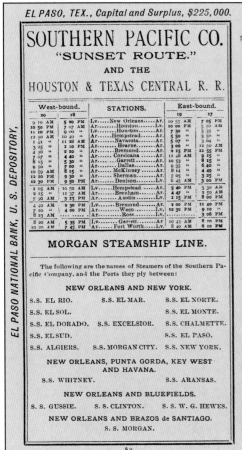

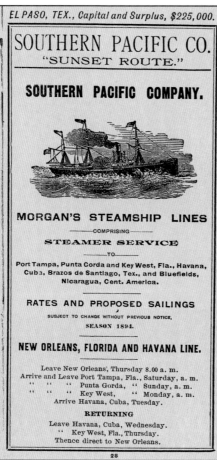

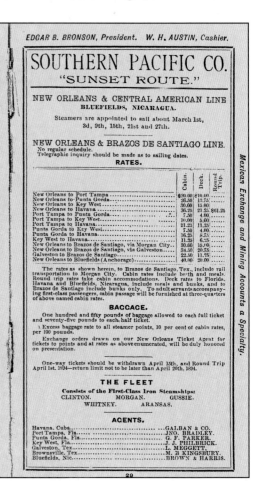

Above: An 1894 Southern Pacific Company timetable for the Gulf States. Besides the extensive steamship routing and its own Sunset Route to Los Angeles, SP was completing its takeover of the Houston and Texas Central Railroad, which provided it with access to central Texas. It also would purchase some small lines that gave it independent access to Galveston, to which it had acquired shared rights in 1881.

Right: The Port of Galveston in 1927 was privately owned by the Galveston Wharf Company, which had been established in 1854 and was one of the largest privately controlled terminal and port companies in the United States. It was acquired by the city of Galveston in 1940.

Right: Hand transfer of cargo from a steamer to a Railway Express car at the Port of Galveston in the 1930s. The Railway Express Agency was formed in 1929 from four major private express companies. From that date until the company was sold in 1969, eighty-six railroads owned the company; their voice in company affairs was in proportion to the amount of express traffic they carried.

Below: A four-wheel yard or maintenance-of-way crane moves timbers in the Louisville & Nashville's Mobile yard in 1895. These cranes were self-propelled, with a top speed of eight to ten mph (12.8–16kph), but could travel only short distances because of the limited amount of coal—for the vertical steam boilers—they could store. The small cranes had lifting capacities of between three and ten tons (3.1–10.2t), had outriggers that could be extended from each side, and employed three drums: one for lifting the boom and the others for operating a bucket or claws as well as for cable movement. Most of them were manufactured by the Brown Hoisting Machinery Company.

The lovely Louisville & Nashville Depot in New Orleans was located at the foot of Canal Street on the Mississippi. Vivien Leigh disembarked from an L&N passenger train at the station in the 1951 movie made from Tennessee Williams' play, fluttered her eyelashes, and said, "They told me to take a streetcar named Desire." The streetcar, now New Orleans Public Service No. 922, still operates, but the L&N station, once one of five in New Orleans, closed with others upon the opening of the New Orleans Union Passenger Terminal in 1954.

Santa Fe and the Texas and Pacific connected with parts of the southwest, and various short lines filled in the gaps. However, besides Southern Pacific, the Illinois Central was the principal railroad entering New Orleans. In 1856 it had opened a line from Chicago to Cairo, Illinois, at the confluence of the Mississippi and Ohio rivers. It then contracted with and eventually controlled steamboat lines sailing to New Orleans and other river ports. Illinois Central (IC) also began buying up other railroads, including the West Feliciana Railroad and the Louisville, New Orleans, and Texas Railroad. These gave the IC lines extending not only to New Orleans but to the important cotton-producing areas of Louisiana, Alabama, Mississippi, and Tennessee. In fact, by the 1890s, the Illinois Central and the Yazoo and Mississippi Valley Railroad, chartered as a sub-

sidiary in 1892 but operated as a separate leased company, together brought to New Orleans one-tenth of the entire cotton crop of the United States. Actually, the two roads could have handled more: because the South's railroad network was still relatively undeveloped compared to the North's, a fair amount of cotton was shipped north rather than south. In 1892 river steamers and barges carried 3,153,261 tons (3,203,713.1t) of freight to New Orleans, while railroads transported 3,980,996 tons (4,044,691.9t).

In the 1890s Galveston was still the most important Gulf port, being the world's foremost shipper of cotton and ranking fifth nationally in tonnage of all cargoes shipped. But in 1900 Galveston suffered a natural calamity from which it would never recover. In that year a terrible storm hit the city, leaving it prostrate at the time when Spindletop—Texas' first big oil gusher—turned Texas into the country's largest petrochemical producer. Houston, always a natural competitor of Galveston's, convinced Congress to appropriate funds to build a fifty-mile (80km) -long ship canal to the Gulf along the old Buffalo Bayou. At its completion in 1914 Houston took over as the Gulf's primary port, a role it never relinquished.

Above: On an apron in New Orleans, 8,000-gallon (30,280l) tank cars are being filled, possibly with coconut oil, in this photograph dating from about 1920. The cars belong to the Palmolive-Peet Company, which perhaps was importing soap base. The only other liquid import into New Orleans at that time was molasses.

Right: Unloading boxes of raisins at one of the Galveston Wharf Company's thirty warehouses. The company also controlled thirty-two piers and five miles (8km) of paved roads. Some of the railroad cars belong to the Galveston, Houston & Henderson Railroad, which from 1856 to 1989 operated under its original charter, not only as a freight belt-line but also as a passenger carrier between Houston and Galveston. After having passed through various ownerships, the GH&H became part of the Missouri Pacific in 1989.

CHAPTER FOUR

THE WEST

U.P.

Oakland's Long Wharf, shown in the early 1900s, was completed by Central Pacific in 1871. Because the area was tidal flats, a two-mile (3.2km) -long pier supported on pilings was needed to reach deep water. The Long Wharf connected passenger trains with steam ferries to San Francisco. Cargo was transferred to and from both sailing vessels and steamers bound for cities across the bay, along the coast, and across the Pacific. The Southern Pacific moved passenger operations to the nearby Oakland Mole in 1882, and the Long Wharf was dismantled in 1919. The vessel in the center is a four-masted barque. The steamer at far left is the *Melville Dollar*. Note the laborious, stick-by-stick handling of lumber.

Southern California

In 1860 Colonel Cyrus Holiday organized the Atchison, Topeka, and Santa Fe Railroad—known until 1863 as the St. Louis and Topeka—to transport cattle from Santa Fe to Kansas City. The colonel, an attorney, former fund-raiser for the Erie Railroad, and past mayor of Topeka, Kansas, also had greater dreams—one might even say grandiose dreams, for his little railroad. Holiday hoped to connect Southern California with the Gulf of Mexico and to connect them both to the new metropolis of Chicago. However, he faced some stiff competition. The Central Pacific Railroad, later to become part of the Southern Pacific, was also building toward Southern California, and it was controlled by some of the most powerful railroad barons in the country. The "Big Four" (Mark Hopkins, Charles Crocker, Leland Stanford, and Collis P. Huntington) were gaining their experience building the western half of the transcontinental railroad (to be completed in 1869), and they would be formidable opponents.

Sunny San Diego had one of the best natural harbors on the Pacific Coast, and its civic leaders badly wanted a railroad to complement their port. By transshipping cargoes from the Orient to the eastern United States, they hoped to become a western transportation power to rival San Francisco. So far, however, their desires had been thwarted. A small line begun in 1845—the San Diego, Gila, and Pacific—attempted to connect the town with Yuma, Arizona, but collapsed in bankruptcy. In 1867 former General John C. Fremont organized the Memphis, El Paso, and Pacific. It too failed, followed by the bankruptcy of the fledgling Texas and Pacific. In 1878 the frustrated San Diego city fathers went to railroad tycoon Jay Gould and begged him to build them a railroad. His answer was a classic: "I don't build railroads, I buy them."

Finally, in 1880, a deal was made with the Santa Fe, which had already succeeded in laying track as far as Needles, close to the southeast border of California. At this point, the Santa Fe's confrontation with its imposing competitor could no longer be avoided. In order to build a line from San Diego to meet the track in Needles, the Santa Fe

One of the little dogs the huge tail wagged. The *Senator Perkins* and two other little steam dummies, all built between 1882 and 1888 by San Francisco's National Iron Works, carried passengers and freight along the quarter-mile (0.4km) length of Pacific Coast Steamship's San Diego Wharf. The company's directors also controlled a much larger railroad, the Pacific Coast Railway, which ran from the port for San Luis Obispo to Los Olivos, a distance of about fifty-five miles (88km). The three-foot (91.2cm) -gauge line was eventually overwhelmed by the Southern Pacific Railroad, but not until 1916. (For more information on Pacific Coast Steamship and the Pacific Coast Company's holdings, see pages 152–68)

needed to cross Southern Pacific's right-of-way. To do that, a Santa Fe engineer had built a crossing frog, which would allow each line to cross the other. But the frog was no sooner installed than the furious SP sent a sheriff to confiscate it. Santa Fe men beat the sheriff to the crossing and removed the frog. After he departed, however, when they went to replace it, they found that the SP had countered by parking a switcher on the crossing, temporarily moving it each time an SP train rolled by. This prevented Santa Fe from replacing the frog and effectively shut down its main line. Later, with the help of their own friendly sheriff menacing the SP's switcher crew, a Santa Fe track gang replaced the frog and from then on guarded it. Finally, after a trackage agreement was reached, in 1885 the Santa Fe brought its first train through from the Midwest to San Diego, entirely on its own tracks. Later the Santa Fe bought out some small lines and connected with Los Angeles. Until 1919, when the San Diego and Arizona Railway was completed to El Centro, there connecting with Southern Pacific, the Santa Fe would have a monopoly in San Diego.

The Southern Pacific, meanwhile, had continued its expansion. In 1870, the Big Four's fledgling railroad had started to put together, through both construction and acqui-

Top: The Santa Monica Long Wharf, shown here shortly after its completion in 1893, was built by the Southern Pacific Railroad in hopes of controlling not only Southern California's rail transport, but also its shipping. The company that controlled the waterfront dictated both the railroads and the shipping lines that could operate there. In 1908, shortly after the congressionally financed expansion of San Pedro harbor was completed, SP discontinued rail service to the Santa Monica wharf, and in 1913 it was dismantled.

Above: Southern Pacific's Daylight, the premier passenger train on the West Coast, ran from Los Angeles to San Francisco. Her northern sister, the Shasta Daylight, continued the journey from San Francisco to Seattle. Powerful streamlined Lima-built 4-8-4s could reach speeds of ninety mph (144kph), and travel time between L.A. and S.F. was often less than ten hours. Here the Daylight heads toward San Francisco along the Pacific Ocean in 1950.

Below and opposite: Because Great Northern Railroad, which operated between the Midwest and Oregon and Washington, had no routes between California and the Northwest, owner James Hill had two speedy vessels built to compete with Southern Pacific's passenger trains traveling from Los Angeles to Portland via San Francisco. While Hill's two vessels operated primarily between Oregon and San Francisco, his *Great Northern* also had winter runs from Los Angeles and San Francisco to Hilo and Honolulu three times a month. This brochure is dated 1915.

sition, a line connecting San Francisco and Los Angeles. It was completed in 1876. The Southern Pacific had also been buying up land in Southern California, principally around the harbor areas of Santa Monica and San Pedro, and by 1890 controlled railroad access to Santa Monica. A new battle was

about to begin to see who would control the ports of Southern California.

Collis Huntington, president of Southern Pacific in 1890, favored Santa Monica as the principal port of Southern California even though SP already was shipping from San Pedro and even though that town had a better natural harbor than did the sleepy resort village to the north. Congress was then debating building a massive breakwater to transform one of the two sites (San Diego was considered too far away from Los Angeles, the major population center) into "the

Right: A San Pedro, Los Angeles, and Salt Lake Railroad express to Salt Lake City awaits passengers at berth 240, San Pedro, in 1909. The railroad, whose name changed to the Los Angeles and Salt Lake in 1916, was absorbed by the Union Pacific in 1921, though final merger approval was not received by the railroad until 1988.

Above: This photograph of San Diego's Santa Fe Wharf was taken in 1910, probably from atop a boxcar. By this time, San Diego Harbor, though growing, was beginning to lag behind San Pedro in size. The age of steam was rapidly overtaking sail. The slower sailing vessels now are being used to go to out-of-the-way destinations or to carry poorly paying cargoes, because they cannot match steam in either speed or dependability.

Above: A San Pedro, Los Angeles & Salt Lake Railroad 2-6-0 in San Pedro, circa 1906. Los Angeles Harbor was initially developed in the 1850s by Phineas Banning, a surveyor who built a wharf on a site he named Wilmington, after his hometown in Delaware. Later he convinced Congress to appropriate funds to connect Dead Man Island (upper right) and Rattlesnake Island (out of photo, to left), to form a breakwater, thus deepening and protecting the harbor. The dredge, upper left, is working on that project. The enlarged island became known as Terminal Island. Owned by the Los Angeles Terminal Railway Company, which ran a line to Los Angeles, it was taken over by the Southern Pacific and eventually by the Los Angeles Port Authority.

Right: A bevy of 0-6-0s await firing up at the San Pedro switching yards on a fall morning in 1924. At left is the municipal fish market, to the right is the E.K. Wood lumber mill, and in the background are a Bethlehem Steel shipyard, Dead Man's Island, and some unidentified U.S. Navy cruisers.

greatest [and] safest harbor on the Pacific Coast, not even excepting San Francisco," as California's Senator John C. Jones put it. Southern Pacific owned so much Santa Monica land (some of it, in fact, purchased from Senator Jones) that if the federal government could be persuaded to spend the enormous amount needed to enclose the exposed harbor, SP would have a railroad monopoly at the most important port in the region.

Opposed to the Santa Monica site was an impressive array of Southern California politicians and landowners who themselves had much to gain if Congress opted to develop San Pedro Harbor. In 1890 Stephen Elkins, secretary of war under President Benjamin Harrison, along with several prominent Los Angeles businessmen, formed the Los Angeles Terminal Railroad Company, which quickly built a line connecting L.A., the San Gabriel Valley, and San Pedro. The Los Angeles Terminal Railroad became the western segment of the San Pedro, Los Angeles, and Salt Lake, which eventually became part of the Union Pacific. Joining the rail-

road's backers were Harrison Gray Otis, owner of the *Los Angeles Times*; John Gaffey, a prominent politician; and the Santa Fe Railroad, who accused SP, in the years of congressional hearings that followed, of trying to create a monopoly. This the SP directors denied. All of Southern California took sides, and the debate in Congress raged for seven years, until finally in 1897 the congressional commission in charge voted in favor of San Pedro.

Meanwhile a truce of sorts had also been reached by Southern Pacific and Santa Fe. They agreed to divide Southern California territory. Santa Fe would have the right to operate over some of SP's tracks. In return Santa Fe promised to support SP's Santa Monica Harbor position. The two railroads nevertheless continued to battle in other ways, undercutting each other in a freight-rate war, much to the delight of farmers and other Southwest shippers. Still, the two railroads had nothing to complain about. For even with the arrival of Union Pacific in 1901, they would split among them one of the largest markets in the United States.

Right: Downtown San Pedro, still sleepy in 1903, with the Southern Pacific freight depot at left. The street at right is the current Harbor Boulevard. The harbor lies off to the left. At the top of the hill is the newly constructed Carnegie Library, just above Plaza Park.

Left: The tramp steamer *Pleiades* unloads lumber at San Pedro in 1903. Across the channel at the Salt Lake Wharf, the steam schooner *San Pedro* is tied up. In the distance a train is carrying rock for the dike that will be the easterly side of Terminal Island after it is filled with dredge spoils. San Pedro, soon to be known as the Port of Los Angeles, was consolidated with the latter city in 1913. San Pedro was located approximately twenty miles (32km) south of downtown Los Angeles. The *Pleiades* has her cargo booms positioned in a married fall with one of each pair over the hatch and the other over the dock. Cables attached to slings of lumber travel through the blocks of both booms, eliminating the need for a boom to swing back and forth between vessel and pier. Note the steam donkey, beside the *Pleiades*' stern, used to move cargo on and off vessels that had no steam-powered winches of their own. Also note the horses that towed dollies of lumber from vessels to rail cars across the wharf.

Right: The S.S. *Columbian*, seen here, was the first ship to visit Los Angeles after sailing through the newly opened Panama Canal (1914). Here she completes loading prior to sailing on to San Francisco. Owned by the American Hawaiian Steamship Company and built in 1913 by WM. Cramp and Sons, Philadelphia, the *Columbian* was 404 feet (122.8m) long, had a 53-foot, 9-inch (16.3m) beam, and displaced 6,262 gross tons (6362.2t). While the *Columbian*'s small wheelhouse provided shelter for the helmsman, her bridge, on which officers and crew had to maintain watch in all weathers, was still completely open. Enclosed bridges were then becoming common on merchantmen and had been incorporated into most liners. Because the U.S. government feared the enemy would destroy the canal during World War I, the waterway was closed the same year it opened and wasn't reopened until 1918.

Above: The railway wharf, Honolulu, in 1913. On the left is the *T J. Harrison*, a cargo ship owned by a trading company. At center is the four-masted schooner *Prosper*. The other vessel is unidentified. The Oahu Railway, which ran from Honolulu three quarters of the way around the island, a distance of seventy-one miles (113.6km), was Hawaii's largest railroad with, at its peak in 1944, a roster of twenty-three locomotives, two diesel electrics, and two homemade, gasoline-powered rail cars. The three-foot (91cm) -gauge line was established by Benjamin Dillingham in 1889.

Above: In 1939, on Oahu Railway's fiftieth anniversary, the engines were polished and edged out of the roundhouse for this special celebration photo. No. 80, the 2-8-2 on the turntable, was a seventy-eight-ton (79.3t) Mikado built by Baldwin Locomotive Works in 1926 and retired in 1948.

Right: Kahului Railroad Company's first locomotive, No. 2 (originally named *Kinau*), poses in 1910 on the wharf at Kahului, Maui, along with the S.S. *Claudine Pierside*. The three-foot (91cm) -gauge Kahului Railroad was the descendant of the Kahului & Wailuku Railroad, the first railroad in Hawaii, established in 1879. It ran along Maui's north shore, serving sugar mills and canneries. The Hawaiian Islands had six narrow-gauge lines and one standard-gauge (the Hilo Railroad) over the years. Now only one, the Lahaina, Kanapali & Pacific, a three-foot-gauge tourist-excursion line, still operates on Maui.

Northern California

It is interesting that the two most important ports, historically, in the United States were the most difficult to reach from adjacent land areas. Manhattan, New York Harbor's focal point, is an island, and San Francisco sits at the end of a peninsula surrounded on two sides by San Francisco Bay and on the third by the Pacific Ocean. So in both cities if you were successful in the railroad business, you were also in the steamship business. While by the 1870s steam-powered vessels were beginning to replace sail on many of the world's major trade routes, the confined ports and harbors—where fuel was easily obtained, where wind was often lacking, and where great maneuverability was critical—were obvious places for using steamers, and they soon proliferated in America's harbors.

The first regular steam ferry to cross San Francisco Bay seems to have been the *Kangaroo*, which in 1850 began sched-

The Hyde Street Pier—one of two San Francisco terminals for ferries going to Sausalito and to Berkeley, Oakland, Richmond, and Alameda—in 1931. Southern Pacific Ferries and its rival, Golden Gate Ferries, had merged two years earlier and shared the Hyde Street terminal with Northwestern Pacific Railroad ferries. Northwestern Pacific, started in 1907 by SP and Santa Fe to operate a rail system along California's sparsely populated north coast, ran ferries to Sausalito and Tiburon. SP purchased Santa Fe's shares in 1929 and became the sole owner.

uled service between San Francisco and Oakland. Competition developed quickly, and by 1858 a score of ferries crisscrossed the bay. But it was not until 1869 that the Central Pacific/Southern Pacific got into the ferry business. It began regular service from the East Coast to San Francisco using Union Pacific track from Ogden, Utah. When the trains reached Oakland, railroad-owned, wooden steam ferries met them and carried passengers the last three and a half miles (5.6km). The famous "Oakland Mole" railroad-ferry terminal opened in 1882, handled hundreds of ferries and trains daily, and operated for nearly eighty years, until it was abandoned in 1960. Ferry service ended in 1958, with buses carrying passengers between Oakland and San Francisco.

By the 1880s the Southern Pacific had a monopoly on standard-gauge transport throughout most of California and was setting its freight rates accordingly. Farmers and ranchers in the great Central Valley, even then California's grain supplier, were up in arms. So were many of San Francisco's prominent and wealthy businessmen, who felt they were being gouged when shipping their products. Together these diverse interests

Right: In 1922 SP advertised four ferry routes: from San Francisco to Oakland, Berkeley, Sausalito, or Tiburon. By 1930, a year after the line acquired its competitor, Golden Gate Ferries, Southern Pacific's ferry business was considered the world's largest. It and its affiliates together operated forty-three boats, which carried nearly fifteen million passengers per year.

Below: The Oakland Pier, always called the Oakland Mole because it was built on a bed of fill dredged from San Francisco Bay, was Southern Pacific's transcontinental terminus; it also handled trains to and from the Northwest and many California destinations. Western Pacific and Santa Fe shared the facilities for many years, as did commuters from many East Bay communities. Travelers ended (or began) their trips by taking one of three SP ferries that operated around the clock, together making more than one hundred trips per day on the 3.3-mile (5.3km) route to San Francisco's Ferry Building.

The Southern Pacific ferry *Berkeley* arrives at the Oakland Mole. These photographs, taken in the late 1950s, represent the end of an era. Ferry service across San Francisco Bay was discontinued in 1958, and shortly thereafter the Mole was demolished to be replaced by a new container port. The *Berkeley* was one of the first double-end propeller-driven steam ferries when she was built in 1898. She was rebuilt in 1917, was 279 feet (84.9m) long, and could accommodate nineteen hundred passengers. The San Francisco–Oakland Bay Bridge is in the background.

decided to build a "people's railroad" running from San Francisco through the Central Valley to Los Angeles. Sugar magnate Claus Spreckels and his family, who were among the largest contributors, also arranged for waterfront land at China Basin for a San Francisco terminal. The cities of Oakland, Stockton, and San Jose contributed, among them, nearly $400,000. The new Valley Railroad grew rapidly. Its tracks reached south to Fresno in 1896, and service began that same year. But almost immediately its backers agreed to let their railroad be taken over by the Santa Fe, which had been questing after a northern California terminus; two were soon developed, at Richmond in 1900 and at Oakland in 1904.

A Santa Fe carfloat heads toward the San Francisco–Oakland Bay Bridge on its way to the Santa Fe switching yard located in China Basin. To the right can be seen the San Francisco skyline with the Ferry Building visible at lower center. The Santa Fe also operated its own fleet of ferries until 1933, at which time its trains began using the Oakland Mole railroad-ferry terminal.

Right: The Santa Fe tug *John Hayden* moves a carfloat from Richmond toward San Francisco. Marin County is in the background. The *John Hayden*, formerly U.S. Army tug *L.T.—830*, was originally steam-powered and was converted to diesel in 1964. She was built in Point Pleasant, West Virginia, in 1945 and retired in 1975.

Above: In 1900 the Atchison, Topeka & Santa Fe completed its line from Southern California to Point Richmond on the northeast shore of San Francisco Bay. Along with a ferry dock the Santa Fe built a large roundhouse and freight yards. Business boomed when Standard Oil established its refinery on adjacent land. Here the Santa Fe tug *Paul Hastings* holds its carfloat in position while a switcher unloads a string of cars at the refinery. Note how the carfloat is stabilized by being pressed against the row of pilings. To prevent shifting, pilings or dolphins (cable-wrapped groupings of pilings) are usually placed on the side of a vessel opposite the direction of prevailng winds or strong currents.

Even with the competition, however, the Central Pacific/Southern Pacific (CP/SP) prospered. Part of the reason was a strategy that it pioneered among American railroads: buying steamship companies. CP/SP's steamships brought huge amounts of cargo to the railroad and at the same time squeezed its competitors. Early on, Central Pacific bought some small steamship companies that were operating paddle-wheelers on the Sacramento and San Joaquin rivers. Its major Pacific Ocean steamship ventures, however, began as a defensive measure.

In 1867, a Pacific Coast steamship giant, Pacific Mail Steamship Company, inaugurated service from the Orient to

Above: The Occidental & Oriental's steamer *Gaelic* (built in 1872, 2,600 gross tons [2641.6t], 370 feet [112.5m]) is shown in an old stephenograph (a type of needlepoint) celebrating her first voyage from Japan to the United States in 1875. Just chartered from the British White Star Line, the *Gaelic* and her sister ships *Oceanic*, *Belgic*—and later the *Arabic*, *Coptic*, and *Doric*—were modern, single-screw steamers that were either ship- or bark-rigged with plenty of sail to assist their compound or triple-expansion steam engines. They operated between San Francisco and (usually) Yokohama, Hong Kong, and Manila. The *Gaelic* flies the "Red Duster," the British maritime ensign. Surrounding the Union crest above her are, from right to left, the O&O house ensign, the U.S. flag, and the British naval ensign. So few foreign merchant ships had visited Japan that their ensigns were often mistakenly identified by the Japanese.

Right: General Ulysses S. Grant returns to North America in September 1880 on Pacific Mail's S.S. *City of Tokyo*. After a two-and-a-half-year world tour with his wife and son, the former president arrives in San Francisco. By 1880 Pacific Mail Steamship and Occidental & Oriental Steamship were both controlled by Central Pacific Railroad, Southern Pacific's predecessor, and formed America's largest trans-Pacific steamship operation.

San Francisco. Since the 1840s Pacific Mail had been operating vessels between New York and California via stagecoach over the isthmus of Panama. After the transcontinental railroad was completed in 1869, Pacific Mail's passengers and freight from Asia bound for eastern U.S. cities could save nearly two weeks going by train instead of by ship via Panama—and for a while this seemed all right with Pacific Mail. Then in 1873 the steamship company drastically cut its freight rates for cargo going between Asia and the East Coast via its Panama route. Within a year Pacific Mail had stolen most of Central Pacific's freight business. The "Big Four" were furious and immediately devised a scheme to retaliate.

Right: The S.S. *Coptic* was larger and newer than the *Gaelic* (4,352 gross tons [4,421.6t], 430 feet [130.7m] by 42 feet [12.8m]). Launched in 1881 by the famous shipbuilders Harland & Wolff of Belfast, she was steel-hulled and was propelled at 15 knots by her compound steam engine. From Hong Kong to San Francisco her average voyage time was about twenty-five days. Besides passengers she carried cargoes of tea, silk, rice, sugar, and opium. Westbound, her major cargoes were flour, silver, Mexican dollars, and manufactured goods.

Above: The S.S. *China* was built in 1889 for Pacific Mail by Fairfield Shipbuilding of Govan, Scotland, to replace the Mail's *City of Tokyo*, lost off the Japanese coast in 1885. The *China* was a newer class of vessel for Pacific Mail—much faster, larger, and more dependable than their old paddle-wheelers. She was 5,600 tons (5,689.6t), 440 feet (133.8m) by 48 feet (14.6m), and powered by a triple-expansion engine. She was capable of 17 knots on steam alone, though, as is evident, her owners still considered sails necessary as backup propulsion.

Together with the Union Pacific Railroad, the Central Pacific created the Occidental and Oriental (O&O) Steamship Company. The new company leased nine vessels, which soon began sailing from San Francisco to the major Asian ports. The O&O offered cargo rates from Asia to New York comparable to Pacific Mail's, with delivery that was much quicker. Ostensibly the Occidental and Oriental was established to regain control of the railroads' freight business, but many knowledgeable people said that it was really established to bring Pacific Mail to its knees.

Although the Occidental and Oriental and other competitors cut deeply into Pacific Mail's revenue, the latter company's coastal shipping and domination of routes to Central America prevented major losses. Still, Pacific Mail suffered. In 1875 it capitulated and agreed to divide the Asian business

Right: By 1907, when this ad appeared, probably in the *Shipping News*, Southern Pacific and its allied companies controlled twenty-two ocean-going vessels, which sailed over nineteen thousand route miles (30,400km). It was the largest railroad-owned shipping empire in the United States and it was still growing.

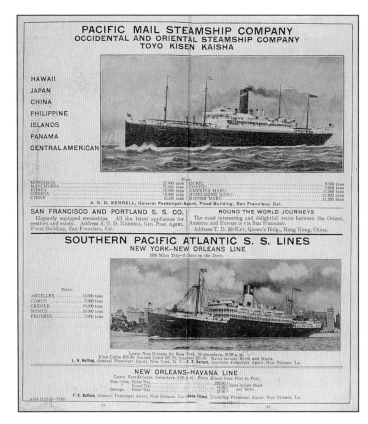

Above: The *Korea* represented the modern transoceanic passenger/cargo liner. She and her sister vessel, the *Siberia*, of 11,300 tons (11,176t) each, entered trans-Pacific service for Pacific Mail in 1902 and easily outclassed any and all competitors. They were built by Newport News Shipbuilding of Virginia, were 551 feet (167.5m) by 63 (19.2m), and their quadruple-expansion engines turning twin screws could propel them at 20 knots, though they usually sailed at 16 knots. Passenger comforts were also far superior to those of most other vessels sailing the Pacific. They were a great success.

with the O&O as well as to transfer all East Coast–bound cargo to the Central Pacific. In 1893 Collis Huntington gained control of Pacific Mail, passing it on to the Southern Pacific when he died in 1900. Thus, at the turn of the century the Southern Pacific Railroad had steamship fleets totaling more than thirty vessels that sailed nearly halfway around the world.

Until 1915, when Southern Pacific divested itself of its Pacific steamship companies, its vessels discharged American manufactured products at Asian ports while loading valuable cargoes of silk, tea, and even opium, which subsequently were

San Francisco coaling dock for the Pacific Mail Steamship Company in the 1870s. With the proliferation of oceangoing steamers in the 1860s and 1870s, sailing vessels, which were much slower, were forced to carry less lucrative cargoes such as coal, which they took to coaling stations up and down the West Coast, to the Hawaiian Islands, and to other Pacific islands. Note the photographer's wagon beneath the coaling platform.

transshipped to points around the United States. Its silk trains, with multimillion-dollar cargoes of silk cocoons or raw silk, were heavily guarded and were given priority over all other trains, even passenger limiteds. Often they set speed records. In 1929, for example, a Southern Pacific/Union Pacific/Chicago and Northwestern silk train made the run from San Francisco to Chicago in an unbelievable forty-nine hours. Direct connections from Asia to Chicago were also incredible for their day. Prior to the ascendancy of air transport, the railroads were America's transportation innovators, and in combined railroad/steamship operations Southern Pacific led the way.

Meanwhile, on San Francisco Bay, the railroad continued its maritime operations. As early as the 1870s it had begun building its own ferries at a shipyard it established on the Oakland estuary. SP ferries plied three main routes to San Francisco, two from Oakland and one from Alameda, carrying commuters and general passengers and freight as well as railroad traffic. Small side-wheel steamers were built to carry railroad cars across the bay. Then in 1879, the railroad completed and placed in service on the Carquinez Straits, at the northeast

Manpower, horsepower, and sail power still predominated on the San Francisco waterfront in 1900, but not for long. The steam-powered winch donkey at right probably uses the vessel's derricks or blocks mounted on its booms to facilitate the loading or discharging of cargo. The low-slung, horse-drawn drays (center) were built to enable manual loading and unloading with the least effort.

end of the bay, the *Solano*, the largest ferryboat in the world. It could carry two whole trains (two locomotives and either 18 passenger cars or 32 freight cars). By 1872 a terminal with ferry slips had been built at the foot of Market Street. In 1896 it was replaced by what would be a San Francisco landmark, the Ferry Building, with its famous clock tower patterned after a cathedral tower in Seville, Spain.

In 1907 the two old rivals, Southern Pacific and Santa Fe, decided on a joint venture. They had already been cooperating on jointly operated track, but now they formed a railroad, the Northwestern Pacific (NWP), to provide service to the heavily forested area north of San Francisco. The NWP acquired a number of small independent lines and received, in the bargain, two ferry terminals at Sausalito and Tiburon, north of San Francisco. At about this time a new player appeared, the Western Pacific.

THE SOLANO

Top left: The Southern Pacific railroad car ferry *Contra Costa*, sister vessel to the *Solano*, was put in service in 1914 and, as it was nine feet (2.7m) longer, at 433 feet (131.6m) overall, usurped the *Solano*'s claim to being the largest ferry in the world.

Bottom left: *Solano* passengers and crew inspect a pair of 4-4-0s. The Southern Pacific engine on the left was built by Cooke Locomotive works in 1864. The engine on the right was also built by Cooke, in 1888. It was operated by Northern Railway, an SP construction line, and eventually became SP1403. The construction of the *Solano* was advanced for her time. She had four Pratt trusses running fore and aft directly under the tracks, stiffening the vessel and fastening her deck to the hull. She was also divided by eleven transverse bulkheads creating a dozen watertight compartments that rendered her very nearly unsinkable. The *Solano* and the *Contra Costa*, also built at Southern Pacific's Oakland yard, ferried trains across the Carquinez Straits, the narrows between San Pablo and Suisun bays, northeast of San Francisco Bay. They not only provided a shortcut for trains bound for the Oakland terminal arriving from Sacramento and points east but also saved a long southern detour through Stockton. Both vessels were retired in 1930 when SP's Martinez–Benicia railroad bridge was completed over the narrows.

Opposite: The *Solano* pulls into the dock at Benicia. The four tracks running her length could hold thirty-six freight cars or twenty-four passenger cars plus two locomotives in each case. By the 1920s, with the increased size of freight cars and especially passenger cars, the ship's capacity had decreased to thirty-two freight or eighteen passenger cars, plus locomotives. The aprons, or bridges, connecting the boat with slips at Port Costa and Benicia were one hundred feet (30.4m) long, had four tracks, and were raised and lowered hydraulically by means of a combination of pontoons and counterweights.

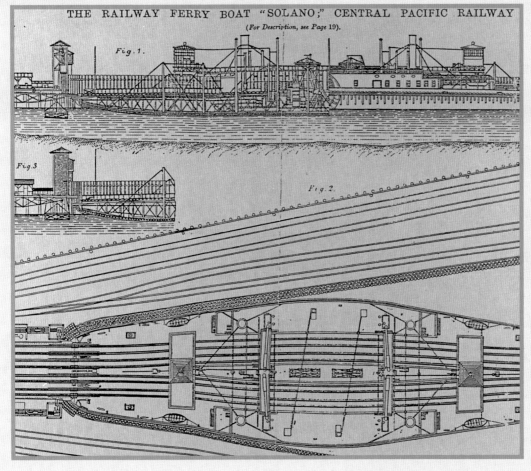

THE RAILWAY FERRY BOAT "SOLANO;" CENTRAL PACIFIC RAILWAY

(For Description, see Page 19).

Fig. 1.

Fig. 3

Fig. 2.

Left: Diagram of Central Pacific-Southern Pacific's side-wheel ferry *Solano*, from the July 1883 edition of *Engineering Magazine*. Then the largest ferry in the world, the *Solano* was built in 1879 at CP's yard in West Oakland. The boat was 424 feet (128.9m) by sixty-four feet (19.5m) by five feet (1.5m) (six feet, six inches [1.9m] draft loaded), carried 8,541 tons (8,677.7t), and was powered by two vertical-beam steam engines, each with one enormous cylinder having a sixty-inch (1.5m) bore and an eleven-foot (3.3m) stroke. The engines were fired from eight 143-tube steel boilers placed in pairs fore and aft of each paddle-box. The two side wheels, thirty inches (76cm) in diameter with twenty-four buckets each, were operated independently to enhance vessel maneuverability. Four eleven-foot, six-inch (15.2cm) -long by five-foot, six-inch (1.7m) -deep rudders were coupled together at each end and operated by hydraulic steering gear from their own steam engines and pumps. Steering was handled in pilot-houses, forty feet (12.1m) above the deck, at each end of the boat.

Above: A Central Pacific
Railroad passenger train
is discharged from the railroad car ferry *Solano* at
Port Costa, California, in
the early 1880s.

Right: A Southern Pacific
switcher loads passenger
cars on the *Solano* at Port
Costa. The twin towers on
either side of the tracks
contain counterweights
and hydraulic engines for
raising and lowering the
100-foot (30.4m) -long float
bridge, or apron. In later
years the bridge was operated by electric motors.
Notice how the track con-
nections between bridge
and vessel seem to be
poorly aligned.

George Gould, the son of railroad tycoon Jay Gould, seemed determined to follow in his father's footsteps. Already he controlled the Missouri Pacific, the Wabash, and the Denver and Rio Grande, but he wanted the first truly transcontinental railroad. Since there was no existing line from Utah to the Coast that he could buy, he decided to build one, completing the Western Pacific in 1909. But building railroads is a risky business, even for tycoons. Gould no sooner had finished his railroad than he realized he would not be able to pay for its enormous cost overruns, and he lost control of it to creditors. For the next quarter-century the Western Pacific staggered from bankruptcy to bankruptcy but somehow managed to keep its cars rolling. It even outwitted the SP, which had previously monopolized the Oakland waterfront. After building a track on dredged bayfront land, the Western Pacific built its own ferry terminal in Oakland and had its own fleet of steamers and carfloats to move passengers and railroad cars to San Francisco. The Western Pacific provided direct competition with SP to Chicago through some of the most scenic regions in the United States.

By 1920 the SP, WP, NWP, and Santa Fe were each operating both railroad-car ferries (Santa Fe used only floats) and passenger ferries across the bay. The Oakland, Antioch, and Eastern, an electric interurban line, also ran gasoline-powered railroad-car ferries across Suisun Bay, to the northeast of San Francisco Bay. The Western Pacific, through purchasing the Sacramento Northern and the Oakland, Antioch, and Eastern subsidiaries, also became heavily involved in electric interurban service. The sixth railroad/ferry combine was also an electric interurban. The San Francisco, Oakland, and San Jose Railway, which became the Key System, connected many East Bay cities, particularly Berkeley and Oakland, with San Francisco on its own ferries. In 1939, when the San Francisco–Oakland Bay Bridge opened, it was Key System

A little 2-4-2T saddle tanker that was built by Baldwin in 1887 poses in 1905 with a forerunner of the San Francisco cable cars. The Ferries and Cliff House Railroad opened in 1887 and went from steam to electric in 1906, just before the great San Francisco fire. It ran from the ferry terminal on the bay to the Cliff House overlooking the Pacific Ocean, became part of the Sutter streetcar line, and was eventually absorbed by the San Francisco Municipal Railway, which is still in existence.

electrics that ran on the bridge's lower deck and spelled doom to the East Bay ferry runs.

The 1920s were the heyday of the ferries. Southern Pacific, the dominant operator, ran thirteen vessels, including the huge railroad-car carrier *Solano* and a newer sister, the *Contra Costa*, launched in 1914. The SP fleet, also operating as an independent subsidiary, known as SP/Golden Gate Ferries, consisted of three railroad-car ferries, ten passenger ferries—some of which also carried automobiles—and five stern-wheel river steamers, which ran to Stockton and Sacramento. Besides these, SP had four tugs, three dredges, and two pile drivers. Calling itself the

Above: A gregarious State Belt engineer and fireman greet the photographer, probably in the 1920s. The State Belt has handled waterfront switching duties from the 1890s to the present, using 0-6-0s before changing to diesels in the 1950s.

Right: This picture shows the view facing north along San Francisco's Embarcadero, then called East Street, May 1906, about three weeks after the earthquake and fire. Note the collapsed buildings on the left. The office of Crowley Maritime, a large tug and barge company, is on the right. The second boxcar from the left belongs to the Oregon Railway and Navigation Company. The name Embarcadero, derived from the Spanish verb *embarcar*, "to embark," was subsequently given not just to the street but to the whole waterfront area. San Francisco was the largest port on the West Coast until overtaken by Los Angeles in the 1920s.

R.R. AND SHIPPING, MAY 11, 1906.

TURRILL & MILLER, OFF. PHOTO.
THE CALIFORNIA PROMOTION COMMITTEE

largest railroad-operated ferry system in the world, it ran not only the two largest railroad-car ferries, but also the two largest passenger ferries, the *Alameda* and the *Santa Clara*. In 1920 its vessels carried nearly thirty-one million passengers and more than 560,000 automobiles.

Most San Francisco ferry traffic came through the Ferry Building's ten slips. Operated by the State of California, it was said to be the busiest terminal in the world, excepting London's Charing Cross station. Indeed, until the 1920s San Francisco was second only to New York as the busiest seaport in the United States. Its Embarcadero docks handled vessels from all over the world. State Belt switchers clanged boxcars opposite the wharves, and row after row of trucks awaited their turns to load or discharge goods. The port was in its heyday.

By 1958, however, the ferries had been replaced by bridge traffic. The fine ocean-crossing passenger liners and break-bulk freighters were on their way out as well. Commercial jet aviation finished off the luxury liners as a means of intercontinental passenger transport. And vast container yards situated in China Basin and in the East Bay, from which thousands of containers are placed on mega-sized container vessels, ended the old San Francisco waterfront's reign as a freighter port. Now high-speed commuter boats whiz by the odd cruise ship and lines of empty docks.

> San Francisco's famous Ferry Building, completed in 1896, the busiest station of any kind in the United States when this photo was taken, sometime in the mid-1920s. Besides serving ferries from six different fleets (Southern Pacific, Santa Fe, Western Pacific, Key System, Northwestern Pacific, and SP-Golden Gate Ferries), it was also the Market Street terminus for streetcars of the Market Street Railway and the San Francisco Municipal Railway.

Right: At Vallejo in 1905 a San Francisco and Napa Valley R.R. interurban awaits passengers from San Francisco disembarking from the Monticello S.S. Co. steamer *Arrow*. The electric interurban line ran from Vallejo to Napa and later to Calistoga. Fast steamers made the connecting run to San Francisco in less than two hours. When the Monticello line was acquired by the Southern Pacific, its vessels joined the Southern Pacific-Golden Gate Ferries fleet.

Below: State Belt No. 7 switching along the San Francisco Embarcadero about 1933; the partially completed Bay Bridge tower is visible in the background. This photograph was taken during the depths of the Depression, and the bystanders at left watching the switchman and yard bull ride the footplates were probably among the legions of the unemployed idling through their days along the waterfront.

❧ The Northwest ❧

Fifteen years after the signing of the Declaration of Independence, Puget Sound, Washington State's vast inland sea, was still unexplored and uncharted. Not until 1792 did Captain George Vancouver of the Royal Navy survey and claim it for Great Britain. Eventually the Northwest Territories were ceded to the United States, but they continued to languish until the early 1850s, when California's gold rush boom provided an instant and enormous market for lumber from the area's then-unbounded forests. Not until the Civil War, however, was the sparsely populated Northwest deemed important enough to connect by rail to the rest of developing America.

In 1870 the Northern Pacific, with bountiful grants of public and Indian land, began constructing a northern transcontinental railroad extending from Lake Superior to Puget Sound. The NP's problems building the line were legion: desolate prairies, the hostility of the Indians whose territories were being invaded, freezing winters, mountainous snowfalls, and the ever-troubling lack of money. Still, the NP persevered through bankruptcies and reorganizations to complete a line to the Pacific Coast.

Meanwhile, from Port Townsend in the north to Olympia in the south, burgeoning port communities bordering Puget Sound vied to be chosen as the railroad's western terminus and thus to ensure their future as the transportation capital of the Northwest. The main contenders were Seattle and Tacoma. Seattle's city fathers were confident their city would be chosen: they had offered the railroad seventy-five hundred

The S.S. *Northern Pacific* and S.S. *Great Northern* were capable of reaching nearly 25 knots, but there was a price to pay. Both ships rolled unmercifully, and on the great swells of the Pacific many passengers spent their twenty-six hours at sea, from San Francisco to the mouth of the Columbia, retching and heaving. The ships were not popular, and after a year they started losing money. Both ships were requisitioned as troop carriers during World War I. The *Great Northern* proved to be the speediest troop carrier in the Atlantic, beating the crossing times of even the *Leviathan* and the *Mauretania*. In 1922 the *Northern Pacific* caught fire and sank. The *Great Northern* became the command ship of Admiral Hilary Jones, commander of the U.S. fleet, and eventually was refitted as a liner in the Admiral Line.

Right: A view of Northern Pacific's Half Moon freight yards alongside Tacoma's Commencement Bay and the longest grain warehouse in the world (2,360 feet [717.4m]). When this photo was taken, about 1910, Northern Pacific's general offices were still located in the turreted building on the hill to the left of Pacific Avenue. They later became the city jail. On the right side of the street is the old city hall; the police department's stables, partially obscured, are just below it.

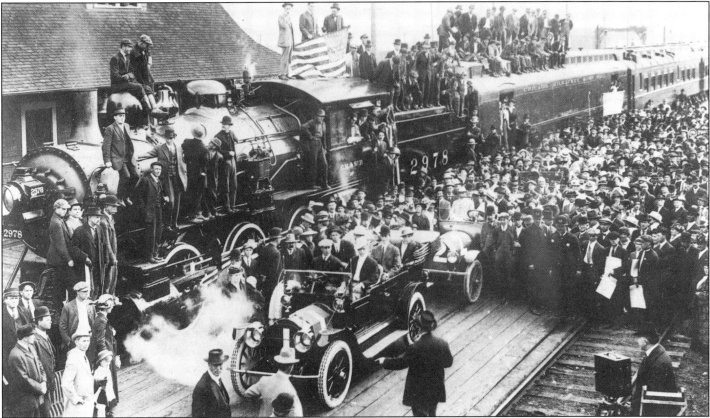

Above: A new railroad comes to town. Tacoma was excited in 1913 when the Chicago, Milwaukee, St. Paul and Pacific completed its transcontinental line from Chicago. The small western city no doubt thought it had reached the apex of America's transportation world. Already served by two transcontinentals, the Northern Pacific and the Great Northern, Tacoma by 1913 not only had attracted the Milwaukee but also had prospects of the Union Pacific from Ogden and the Southern Pacific coming up the coast from California. The city fathers must have had dreams of becoming another San Francisco. But it was not to be.

town lots, three thousand acres (1,212ha) of land, $200,000 in bonds, and $50,000 in cash. How could any competitor match that? In 1873 Seattle's representatives learned to their dismay that Tacoma, the successful bidder, had offered the railroad more than half its town, including most of the shoreline.

Other western communities also wished to become a terminus of the transcontinental railroad. Prominent among these was Portland, in Oregon Territory, and it had taken measures to make sure it would not be left out. Portland's champion was a brilliant young German immigrant, Henry Villard. Villard had been a successful journalist, covering the Lincoln-Douglas debates and Lincoln's presidential nomination before moving to the Northwest. There, he switched careers, and together with American and European partners, he formed the Oregon Railway and Navigation Company. It proceeded to build a line along the Columbia River to Portland to tie into Northern Pacific's transcontinental. But in 1881 Villard's group of investors took on a much greater challenge: control of the bankrupt NP and the completion of the northern transcontinental. In 1883 the rejuvenated NP finally complet-

ed its route from St. Paul, Minnesota, to Portland, Oregon, and then on to Tacoma.

The dynamic Villard wasn't finished, however. In 1882 his group, now operating as the Oregon Improvement Company, had bought a controlling interest in the Pacific Coast Steamship Company, a firm that operated eight small wooden steamers along the California coast. Immediately, Villard expanded the company. Two large iron steamers were ordered. Others were purchased secondhand. Small independent railroads were acquired in California and Washington. The Puget Sound Shore Railroad was to connect Seattle with Tacoma. The Columbia and Puget Sound, formerly the Seattle and Walla Walla Railroad, was to join Seattle and eastern Washington. In 1890 the company bought the Port Townsend Southern to link Port Townsend with Quilcene, and the Olympia and Chehalis Valley Railroad to connect southern and central Puget Sound. Coal and timber lands were also bought with the idea of building a Northwest resource and shipping empire. However, in 1895 the western comet crashed: Oregon Improvement went

By 1916 dining cars were a part of almost every railroad's elite trains, or "limiteds," and the quality of their food became a major selling point. Northern Pacific promoted itself as the "Route Of The Great Big Baked Potato," a popular restaurant item. On its Seattle parade float, Northern Pacific's baked potato looks more like a big hot dog, but there is no mistaking the fish in the tank or the foul-weather-clad fisherman beside it advertising that "Every day is salmon day."

Top: Pacific Coast Steamship's vessel *Umatilla*—328 feet (99.7m), 3,069 tons (3,118.1t)—built in 1881 by John Roach & Sons, Chester, Pennsylvania. The Pacific Coast S.S. Company was probably the only major transportation company in American history whose shipping business was more extensive than its railroad interests. Pacific Coast's steamship routes stretched from north of Juneau, Alaska, to Mazatlán, Mexico—with calls at every major port along the way. In 1893, after the demise of Henry Villard's Oregon Improvement Company, which had taken control of Pacific Coast S.S. in 1881, ownership of the company, now called the Pacific Coast Company, reverted to its founders and agents, Goodall, Perkins & Company. By 1897 the company operated twenty-one vessels over six Pacific Coast routes.

Above: The steamer *Beaver*, 4,500 tons (4,572t), with berths for 378 passengers, and her sister ship, the *Bear*, both entered service in 1910 for Edward Harriman's Union Pacific/Southern Pacific-controlled San Francisco & Portland Steamship Company. Along with the *Rose City*, formerly the U.S. Army transport *Lawton*, they sailed between Astoria (with rail connection to Portland), San Francisco, and Los Angeles. Harriman had started the S.F. & Portland S.S. in 1904 with three smaller vessels. The company became a major Pacific Coast competitor and was in business for twenty years until, due to the antitrade restrictions of the Panama Canal Act, SP was forced to divest itself of S.F. & Portland interests (and SP and UP were split up) in 1914. A subsidiary, the Portland and Coos Bay S.S. Company, which had operated the two-hundred-ton (203.2t) iron steamer *Breakwater*, had previously ceased operations.

The two Great Northern Pacific vessels definitely were not floating palaces compared to their Long Island Sound counterparts. However, the *Great Northern* and *Northern Pacific* did, for a few years, allow James Hill to compete with Southern Pacific's San Francisco–Portland passenger trains. Ship travel time between San Francisco and Flavel (just outside Astoria) on the southern bank of the Columbia River was slightly longer than SP's San Francisco–Portland time when adding the three-and-a-half-hour Spokane, Portland & Seattle Railway connection between Flavel and Portland. The two vessels each made six round-trips a month.

into receivership and was taken over by a new entity, the Pacific Coast Company.

This early transportation conglomerate had acquired Pacific Coast Mail and its six steamers. With sixteen vessels, routes ranging from Canada to Mexico, ownership of the San Diego wharf, and direct connections to the Midwest on Northern Pacific, the new transportation company was dominant in the Northwest—but only for a while.

A new competitor had quietly been working his way west. James Hill, the "Empire Builder," started as a steamboat agent in the Midwest, then bought a steamboat company, then a small railroad, the St. Paul and Pacific. Hill, one of the shrewdest of the railroad tycoons, began fulfilling his dream of a railroad to the Pacific by carefully plotting the least expensive route to build and by routing his line, now called the Great Northern, from one profitable cargo area to the next—from St. Paul and Duluth on Lake Superior to the great grain fields of Minnesota and North Dakota, to the untapped coal fields of Montana, to the timber wealth of the Northwest—and finally to the Pacific.

By the 1880s Seattle's city fathers were desperate for a transcontinental railroad of their own; not surprisingly, they gave generously of their land and harbor to secure the Great Northern terminus, which Hill established on the shores of Elliot Bay. The Great Northern began running through-trains to Seattle in 1893. It had already expanded north along Puget Sound to Vancouver, Canada, by buying the New Westminster and Southern Railway in 1891. To its holdings it added the Seattle and Montana (1898) and the Seattle and Northern, leading to the port of Anacortes, in 1902. Still the Empire Builder wasn't satisfied, and he went back into the shipping business.

Early on, Hill realized that he would not have enough freight to or from the sparsely populated Puget Sound region, but Seattle's fine harbor and its proximity to the Orient provided another source of revenue. In 1896 Hill contracted with the Nippon Yusen Kaisha line of Japan, and that year began the first regular steamship service across the Pacific. Soon after, Hill built the *Dakota* and the *Minnesota*, two 14,000-ton (14,224t) cargo/passenger liners, the largest then afloat; in 1906 he started his own service, the Great Northern Steamship Co., to Yokohama, Manila, and Hong Kong. As previously mentioned, Hill had been in the steamship business earlier. In 1888 he had inaugurated the Northern Steamship Company on the Great

Above: The S.S. *Dakota*, one of Great Northern's twin flag carriers, outbound from Yokohama on a clear day, March 3, 1907, hit a well-charted reef a mile (1.6km) from shore. Passengers and crew were evacuated before she came to rest, half submerged but a total loss. The *Dakota* and the *Minnesota*, at 630 feet (191.5) by 73 feet (22.2m) and weighing 20,718 gross tons (21,049.5t), were then the largest ships to have been built in the United States and to sail under its flag. Each was driven by a pair of triple-expansion steam engines fired by coal-burning boilers, could accommodate more than eighteen hundred passengers, and had thirty-four derricks operated by electric winches. Unfortunately, their speed was only twelve and a half knots.

Right: Following the sinking of the *Dakota* in 1907, the *Minnesota* was the Great Northern's only trans-Pacific carrier (with the exception of the Great Northern Pacific Steamship Company's vessel *Great Northern* sailing to Hawaii). The *Minnesota* made forty sailings to the Orient between 1907 and 1915. She was then sent to Europe with a cargo of food. After breaking down en route she was sold to the Atlantic Transport Company and was scrapped after the war.

1167. Steamship Minnesota, Oriental Liner, Seattle.
Length 630 ft. Capacity 23,000 long tons, equal to 100 trains of 25 cars.

281. NORTHERN PACIFIC, "F

Left: "Short Route To The Orient": "The Great Circle Track route of the 'Minnesota' to the Orient is 500 miles [800km] shorter than any other. From Seattle to Yokohama the distance is 4,280 miles [6,848km], the ship's path following the course of the warm Japan current toward the Aleutian Islands and the Behring Sea. That it takes a short-cut is easily seen by investigation. On the average map, North America and Asia are placed as if they faced each other in an almost parallel position, whereas, in fact, the spherical contour of the globe makes the Asiatic shore-line almost a continuation or projection of the American shore-line to the other side of the globe. Thus the most direct route to Japan or China, instead of being westerly by way of the Sandwich Islands, is northerly past

TING PALACE OF THE PACIFIC," G. N. P. S. S. CO.

Puget Sound and the Behring Sea. It is approximately 1,250 miles [2,000km] further from San Francisco, westerly by way of Hawaii to Yokohama, Shanghai or Hong Kong, than from Puget Sound northerly to the same destinations.

"To give the same thought another expression. The round-trip to the Orient by way of Hawaii is 2,500 miles [4,000km] longer than the Puget Sound round-trip by way of Behring Sea and the Great Circle Track. This is equivalent to a week's voyage for a 15-knot vessel, or nearly nine days at twelve knots.

"The Great Northern Steamship Company in connection with the Great Northern Railway or Northern Pacific Railway, offers not only the shortest and quickest route to the Orient, but adds to this, travel accommodations of such unusual merit that the most discriminating passengers give this route the preference.

"President Taft selected the 'Minnesota' for his trip to the Philippines and many of the foremost statesmen, government offi-cials, army officers, business and professional men, who appreciate and demand the best of everything, prefer the 'Minnesota' for their Trans-Pacific journey."

—Great Northern Steamship Co. brochure

Above: The Great Northern Pacific, Hill's Pacific Coast steamship company, operated the vessels *Northern Pacific* (Hill had taken control of that railroad by 1902) and *Great Northern* on the Pacific Coast only from 1915 to 1917. The *Great Northern* was the first passenger ship to sail through the newly opened Panama Canal in 1914. During their entire existence the two twenty-three-knot ves-sels broke speed records, among them the record from Los Angeles to Honolulu. The 524-foot (159.3m) *Great Northern* and *Northern Pacific* each could carry eight hundred passengers in first-class luxury and a crew of two hundred.

Lakes with two palatial passenger steamers, operating between Minneapolis and Buffalo, and six steel freighters (sold in 1903). In 1914 these companies were joined in the Great Northern Pacific Steamship Company. Hill established this shipping line with his old competitor, the Northern Pacific (which Hill had taken control of in 1893), to provide competition to the Southern Pacific and Union Pacific's San Francisco and Portland Steamship Company, which operated three liners between Portland, San Francisco, and Los Angeles. In 1915 Great Northern Steamship launched two new twenty-three-knot, 856-passenger liners—considered to be among the finest in the world—to run alongside two older vessels between Flavel, Oregon (near Astoria), and San Francisco. Meanwhile, Southern Pacific, after fifty years in the Pacific Coast steamship business and having already phased out its Occidental and Oriental, closed its Pacific Mail Steamship Company. SP gave as its reason Congress' passing of the La Follette Seamen's Act, which, while improving sailors' working conditions, eliminated foreign crews and significantly increased shipping owners' expenses.

At the same time that Hill was building his first transpacific steamship company, he was joining forces with the Northern Pacific on another venture: to acquire the Chicago, Burlington, and Quincy Railroad, which ran from Chicago through the Great Lakes region and, more importantly, south to the Gulf of Mexico. Hill then had the empire he had dreamed of. His tea-and-silk trains highballed east, faster than passenger specials, carrying those cargoes his fleet had brought from the Far East. Cotton, coal, grain, and manufactured goods sped in the other direction, making Hill a fortune and turning little Seattle into one of the most important ports in the country.

The Northern Pacific and Great Northern had other competitors eventually in the Puget Sound region: the Union Pacific–controlled Oregon Short Line from Idaho via Portland, and the Milwaukee Road, which in 1909 complet-

There was hardly room for a hay wagon on Railroad Avenue, Seattle's waterfront, in 1904. The Great Northern and Northern Pacific still controlled most of the right-of-way but leased track to other railroads. Consequently the waterfront was a dangerous jumble of switches, crossings, small stations, and sidings. In 1911 the new Port of Seattle's commissioners began condemnation proceedings in order to purchase and control the waterfront, subsequently establishing a state-owned belt-line switching operation. By that time passenger service already had been moved to Seattle's new King Street Station.

Opposite: The Puget Sound and Grays Harbor R.R. in 1889, probably on the outskirts of Westport. Grays Harbor is Washington State's largest bay outside Puget Sound, and in the 1880s its ports were already thriving, shipping lumber to California, though at that time they had no railroad connections. The P.S. & G.H.R.R did not reach Aberdeen and Hoquiam until 1910. In 1914 the Milwaukee gained access by leasing track from Oregon-Washington R.R. and Navigation (a railroad holding company). Eventually Northern Pacific and Union Pacific also served the area via lines through Centralia. In 1907 the Spokane, Portland, and Seattle acquired the Astoria and Columbia River R.R., which gave it connections to Astoria on the south bank of the Columbia River.

Below: By the time these panoramas of Seattle's waterfront were taken, probably 1901 or 1902, the Oregon Improvement Co. was no more. In the panic of 1893 all Henry Villard's companies had gone bankrupt. James Hill and the Great Northern took over the Northern Pacific, and Oregon Improvement was reorganized as the Pacific Coast Steamship Company. The new company also controlled Pacific Coast Mail (not to be confused with SP's Pacific Mail S.S. Co.), and the two operated vessels from Alaska to Mexico and everywhere in between. Pacific Coast S.S. had also taken control of some of Villard's short-line railroads operating in Oregon and Washington. The side-wheel packet *T.J. Potter*, pictured here, was built in 1888 and operated for much of her life on the lower Columbia River between Portland, Oregon, and Ilwaco on the coast. She was laid up in 1916. The prominent building seen above *Potter*'s pilothouse is the King County Courthouse, built in the 1890s.

ed its line from Missoula, Montana, to Tacoma and began running through-trains to Minneapolis, St. Paul, and Chicago. The Milwaukee Road (it was then known in the West as the Chicago, Milwaukee, and Puget Sound) also bought local lines running from Bellingham north to Canada and from Port Angeles to Port Townsend and Port Ludlow on Washington's Olympic Peninsula. To join those disconnected segments the railroad developed its own marine division of tugs and carfloats. That is gone now. But other railroad-car ferry operations continue on. The Burlington Northern Santa Fe, the Union Pacific, and the Alaska Railroad currently load carfloats destined for Alaska and, in the case of the Union Pacific, also for the Canadian National in British Columbia. The railroad-car ferry operations still play a small but vital role in north-western transportation.

Top: In 1905 Great Northern's Oriental Limited steamed past Great Northern's Pacific "fleet," the *Dakota* and the *Minnesota*, alongside Great Northern's Seattle wharf, grain elevator, and warehouses. James Hill's transportation conglomerate was one of two on the Pacific Coast. His only match was Southern Pacific's rail and shipping empire to the south.

Above: Milwaukee's Seagoing Railroad Company probably wished it had stayed on shore when this picture was taken. The barge *MT* sits with a load of overturned cars, probably the result of adverse weather crossing

Puget Sound. The Milwaukee Road's barge subsidiary, begun in 1909, operated up to seven carfloats with capacities of from two to twenty-one freight cars and sailed to nearly every railroad port in Puget Sound that Milwaukee could not reach on her own tracks. Normally one or two barges were towed at the end of an eight-hundred-foot (243.2m) -to-twelve-hundred-foot (364.8m) cable, depending on weather, with an additional one-hundred-foot (30.4m) to 150-foot (45.6m) line between two barges. At rear is the 118-foot (35.9m), 900hp tug *Milwaukee*. Built in 1913, she was then the largest tug on the Pacific Coast—the pride of the fleet.

Right: A Milwaukee Road SD-9 brings cars off the carfloat dock at Port Townsend in Puget Sound shortly before operations ceased due to bankruptcy in 1977. A fifty-one-mile (81.6km) stretch of line between Port Angeles and Port Townsend servicing the timber and paper industry sprang to life three years later as the independent Seattle and North Coast Railroad, which proclaimed itself the only American railroad that operated by tidal flow. With only three very used diesels and two old barges, the S&NC struggled for four years, sailing to and from Seattle, before it too went under in 1984.

Below: A Northern Pacific passenger train skirts Puget Sound on its way to Portland in 1968. From 1926 to 1971, when Amtrak took over passenger service, Great Northern, Northern Pacific, and Union Pacific pooled their service, each sending one train north and south once a day.

Left: A construction crane unloads supplies in Anchorage in 1917 for Alaska's new railroad, then under construction, from Anchorage and Seward to Fairbanks. The road finally opened in 1923 with 470 miles (752km) of mainline after severe winters, rail warping caused by the shifting tundra, and other arctic difficulties slowed construction.

Top: Operational maintenance was and still is a nightmare. In the winter 10- to 15-foot (3–4.6m) snowfalls are not uncommon in some areas, requiring constant use of rotary plows pushed by two locomotives, as seen in this photo taken just outside the Anchorage yards. Avalanches occur nearly every winter and spring. Patrols must precede trains to spot not only the avalanches, but any ice that has accumulated on the tracks—or errant moose, often weighing over twelve hundred pounds (543.6kg) each. Per-mile maintenance costs are higher than those of any major U.S. line, and still the Alaska Railroad keeps rolling.

Above: Dockside services have changed since 1917. In 1955 a floating crane unloads new passenger cars for the Alaska Railroad, one of the few in the United States totally dependent on maritime connections for survival. Ownership of the railroad was transferred in 1985 from the U.S. government to the state of Alaska. In that year the railroad operated fifty-seven diesel engines, forty-six passenger cars, and 1,439 freight cars over a total of 655 miles (1,048km) of track.

CHAPTER FIVE
MODERN
OPERATIONS

Matson Navigation Company's container ship *R.J. Pfeiffer* is pictured here on her way to Hawaii. The *Pfeiffer*, 713 feet (216.8m) long and 27,100 deadweight tons (27,533.6t), was built in 1992. She can carry approximately sixteen hundred containers and can load them in about a day and a half. She and Matson's other vessels sail principally between Hawaii and West Coast ports. Matson is one of the few major U.S. flag carriers still sailing.

The 1930s saw the first glimmers of another revolution in rail and ship transport. As road networks across America improved, truckers began taking substantial business from the railroads. Diesel engines started to replace steam locomotives. Cargo ships became larger and faster, with more hold capacity and high-speed winches. But the most profound change, which would turn both shipping and railroads upside down, went unnoticed outside the industry. In 1930 the Pennsylvania Railroad began putting shipping containers on flatcars instead of loading items piecemeal into boxcars. The Interstate Commerce Commission quickly squashed the fledgling container program as being unfair to truckers—and for a while containerization progressed no further.

Still, industry heads had turned to watch the Pennsylvania experiment and the few that followed it. Railroad executives realized that there were advantages to using the new shipping containers. Once filled at the factory, they could be loaded on a railcar in minutes instead of tying up the car for days, and an entire train might be loaded in one location, eliminating hundreds of switching operations and untold expenses.

Shipowners saw the potential for even greater savings. Often freighters sat loading or discharging in a single port for two or three weeks. In some congested harbors a vessel would sometimes lie idle for months while awaiting a berth. The costs to shipowners and to shippers had become staggering, and both eagerly sought ways to reduce delays.

Piggybacking, or intermodal operations, as it is now called, actually dates back to the nineteenth century. Sections of canal boats, complete with cargo, were hauled on flatcars in Pennsylvania from 1843 to 1855 as part of the Pittsburgh to Philadelphia rail-canal route of the Allegheny Portage Railway. In Canada and on Long Island, farm trains were

A top loader places a container on a double-stack rail car at the Port of Tacoma. Between them, the ports of Tacoma and Seattle handled 1,440,000 containers in 1996, and most of those either came or left by rail. In fact, the intermodal rail car, a sample of which is shown here, has replaced the boxcar as the standard freight car of the American railroads.

A Norfolk Southern switcher moves a Triple Crown car through a yard. The cars, with a single pair of railway wheels that drop down when needed, are equally at home on the highway and on rails. Strung together, they can operate economically over rail lines for distances of up to 400 miles (640km), instead of requiring their own highway tractors or intermodal cars. This is simply one example of the evolution of intermodal technology.

loaded with teams and wagons in the 1880s to save the farmers long drives to market. And, of course, circuses carried their wagons, then trucks, aboard the famous circus trains for more than a century. But it wasn't until 1950 that container and intermodal transport arrived to stay.

It didn't come cheaply, however. Containerization required enormous capital expenditures. Railroads had to develop new cars, loading equipment, and highway trailers. For shipowners conversion was exponentially more expensive. At first containers were carried as deck cargo on modified conventional freighters and loaded with ship's gear. But this process was slow and unwieldy. In 1958 Sea Land Service Inc. pioneered regular container service on the East Coast, and Matson Lines followed two years later on the West Coast. Giant container, or gantry, cranes soon appeared, but often the old piers could not support the weight of the loading equipment and containers. Nor did they have space to store them, so expensive new port areas had to be developed. People problems also abounded. The longshoremen's unions, incensed at the number of lost jobs, fought tooth-and-nail against the new technology. But they couldn't stop it—nothing could. Still, the idea had come too late to save many shipping companies and railroads. The postwar years were terrible for them both.

The years following World War II had brought cut-rate competition from foreign vessel operators whose costs were a fraction of those borne by their American competition. As a result, U.S. shipping companies, one after another, faced bankruptcy. In the railroads' case, competition from the trucking industry and ICC rate regulation forced hundreds of money-losing railroads to either fold or merge with healthier allies. By 1970, 22 percent of American railroads had gone under, and by 1993 twelve lines controlled 90 percent of the rail business in America. The new technology and the Staggers Bill, which in 1980 deregulated the railroads and allowed them to compete on even terms with the truckers, saved the rest and allowed them to be profitable once more.

Now, two-hundred-car container trains crisscross the United States, forming the "land bridge" that Great Northern's James J. Hill had prophesied a century earlier would one day link Europe and Asia via America's ports. The ports themselves have changed as well. Railcars are unloaded in minutes at enormous container docks filled with mountains of steel boxes; seven-hundred-foot (212.8m) -long container ships load a thousand containers in a day, then speed to their destinations at more than twenty knots. A whole new world of railroad/shipping technology has arrived. But, sadly, it has replaced the bustling ports, the old-fashioned steamships, and the huffing locomotives that once were so much a part of coastal America.

BIBLIOGRAPHY

BOOKS

Abdill, George B. *Civil War Railroads*. New York: Bonanza Books, 1961

Ault, Phil. *Whistles Round the Bend: Travel on America's Waterways*. New York: Dodd, Meade & Company, 1982

Beebe, Lucius, and Charles Clegg. *Hear the Train Blow: A Pictorial Epic of America in the Railroad Age*. New York: E. P. Dutton & Co., Inc., 1952

Benson, Richard W. *Steamships and Motorships of the West Coast*. Seattle: Superior Publishing, Co., 1968

Best, Gerald M. *Railroads of Hawaii*. San Marino, Calif.: Golden West Books, 1978

———. *The Story of The Pacific Coast Company*. Berkeley, Calif.: Howell-North Books, 1964

Bendersky, Jay. *Brooklyn's Waterfront Railways*. New York: The Weekend Chief Publishing Co., 1988

Bergersky, Jr., Arthur W. *Confederated Mobile*. Jackson, Miss.: University Press of Mississippi, 1991

Bonavia, Michael Robert. *The History of the Southern Railway*. Unwin Hyman, 1987

Bramson, Seth. *Speedway to Sunshine*. Boston Mills, Ont.: Boston Mills Press, 1984

Brooks, Terrence. *Pennsylvania Railroad: The Early Days*. Trans-Anglo Books, 1964

Burgess, George H., and Miles C. Kennedy. *Centennial History of The Pennsylvania Railroad Company, 1846—1946*. Philadelphia: The Pennsylvania Railroad Co., 1949

Burke, Padraic. *A History of The Port of Seattle*. Seattle: Port of Seattle, Washington, 1976

Condit, Carl W. *The Port of New York*. Chicago: University of Chicago Press, c.1980

Cudany, Brian J. *Over and Back: The History of Ferry Boats in New York Harbor*. New York: Fordham University Press, 1990

Conway's History of the Ship. *The Golden Age of Shipping: The Classic Merchant Ship, 1900—1960*. London: Conway Maritime Press, 1994

Current, Richard N. *"The Civil War Era: 1848—1873," The History of Wisconsin*, Vol. 2. State Historical Society of Wisconsin, 1976

Demoro, Harre W., and Vernon J. Sappers. *Rails to San Francisco Bay*. New York: Quadrant Press, Inc., 1992

Deverell, William. *Railroad Crossing: Californians and the Railroad 1850—1910*. Berkeley, Calif.: University of California Press, 1994

Douglas, George H. *All Aboard! The Railroad in American Life*. New York: Marlowe and Company, 1995

Douglas, George H. *Rail City: Chicago U.S.A.* La Jolla, Calif.: Howell-North Books, 1981

Drury, George H. *The Historical Guide to North American Railroads*. Wankesha, Wisc.: Kalmbach Publishing Co., 1985

Fitch, Edwin M. *The Alaska Railroad*. Frederick A. Praeger, Publishers, 1967

Fowler, William M., Jr. *Boston Looks Seaward*. Boston: Northeastern University Press, 1985 (orig. pub. by Boston Port Authority, 1941)

Gibbs, Jim, and Joe Williamson. *Maritime Memories of Puget Sound*. West Chester, Penn.: Schiffer Publishing, Ltd., 1987

Gilbert, Paul, and Charles Lee Bryson. *Chicago And Its Makers*. Chicago: Felix Mendelsohn, Publisher, 1929

Gordon, John Steele. *The Scarlet Woman of Wall Street*. New York: Weidenfeld & Nicolson, 1988

Harlow, Alvin F. *Steelways of New England*. New York: Creative Age Press, 1946

Herr, Kincaid. *The Louisville & Nashville Railroad: 1850—1963*. Louisville, Ken.: Public Relation Dept., L.& N., 1964

Hilton, George W. *The Great Lake Car Ferries*. Berkeley, Calif.: Howell-North, 1962

Hitchman, James H. *A Maritime History of the Pacific Coast, 1540—1980*. New York: University Press of America, 1990

Hofsommer, Don L. *The Southern Pacific, 1901—1985*. College Station, Tex.: Texas A&M University Press, 1986

Hollingsworth, Brian. *Atlas of World Railways*. New York: Everest House Publishers, 1980

Hubbard, Freeman. *Encyclopedia of North American Railroading: 150 Years of Railroading in the United States and Canada*. New York: McGraw-Hill Book Company, 1981

Hungerford, Edward. *Men of Erie*. New York: Random House, 1946

Hungerford, Edward. *Men and Iron: The History of the New York Central*. New York: Random House, 1946

Johnson, Harry, and Frederick Lightfoot. *Maritime New York*. Mineola, New York: Dover Publications, 1980

Kemble, Haskell, John. *A Hundred Years of the Pacific Mail*. Mariners' Museum, 1950

Lash, Jefferey N. *Destroyer of the Iron Horse: General Josheph E. Johnston and Confederate Rail Transport, 1861—1865*. Kent, Ohio: Kent State University Press, 1991

Lawson, Will. *Pacific Steamers*. Glasgow: Brown, Son & Ferguson, Ltd., 1927

Lewis and Dryden. *Marine History of the Pacific Northwest: 1800—1895*. Seattle, Wash.: Superior Publishing Co., 1967 (reprint)

Magden, Ronald and A.D. Martinson. *The Working Waterfront: The Story of Tacoma's Ships and Men*. Tacoma, Wash.: Port of Tacoma, A Municipal Corp., 1982

Mann, Robert W. *Rails 'Neath the Palms*. Pennington, New Jersey: Darwin Publications, 1983

Martin, Albro. *Enterprise Denied: Origins of the Decline of American Railroads, 1897—1917*. New York: Columbia University Press, 1971

———. *Railroads Triumphant*. New York: Oxford Press, 1992

Martin, Sidney Walter. *Florida's Flagler*. Athens, Georgia: The University of Georgia Press, 1977 (reprint)

McAdam, Roger Williams. *The Old Fall River Line*. New York: Stephen Daye Press, 1955 (reprint)

McCurdy, H.W. *Marine History of the Pacific Northwest: 1885—1965*; Seattle, Wash.: Superior Publishing, Co., 1966

McLaurin, Meton, and Michale Thomason. *Mobile: The Life and Times of a Great City*. Mobile, Alabama: Windsor Publications, Inc., 1981

Merk, Frederick. *Economic History of Wisconsin During the Civil War Decade*. State Historical Society of Wisconsin, 1916

Meyer, Jacob George Arnold. *Modern Locomotive Construction*. New York: Wiley, 1899

Nesbit, Robert C. *"Urbanization and Industrialization: 1873-1893," The History of Wisconsin*, Vol. 3. State Historical Society of Wisconsin, 1985

O'Connor, George Watson. *Railroads of New York: A Picture Story of Railroading In and Around New York City*. New York: Simmons-Boardman Publishing Corp., 1949

Olson, Sherry H. Balitmore: *The Building of an American City*. Baltimore, Maryland: John Hopkins University Press, 1980

Prince, Richard, E. *Seaboard Air Line Railway*. Millard, Nebraska: R.E. Prince, 1969

———. *Norfolk Southern Railroad, Old Dominion Line and Connections*. Millard, Nebraska: R.E. Prince, 1972

———. *Central of Georgia Railway and Connecting Lines*. Millard, Nebraska: R.E. Prince, 1976

———. *Norfolk & Western Railway, Pocahontas Coal Carrier*. Millard, Nebraska: R.E. Prince, 1980

South Carolina State Ports Authority. *History of the South Carolina State Ports Authority*. Charleston, South Carolina, 1991

Spangenbery, Ray, and Diane Moser. *The Story of America's Railroads*. New York: Facts on File Inc., 1991

Schwantes, Carlos A. *Railroad Signatures across the Pacific Northwest*. Seattle, Wash.: University of Washington Press, 1993

Stover, John F. *History of the Baltimore and Ohio Railroad*. West Lafayette, Ind.: Purdue University Press, 1987

Stover, John F. *History of the Illinois Central Railroad*. New York: MacMillan Publishing Co. Inc., 1975

Swengel, Frank M. *The American Steam Locomotive*. Chicago: Midwest Rail Publications, 1967

Tate, Mowbray E. *Transpacific Steam: The Story of Steam Navigation from the Pacific Coast of North America to the Far East and the Antipodes, 1867—1941*. Cranberry, New Jersey: Cornwall Books, 1986

Various. *Fifty Years of Railroading: 1940—1990*. Wankesha, Wisc.: Kalmbach Publishing Co., 1990

Vela Lee, and Maxine Edwards. *Reaching for the Sea: The Story of the Port of Houston*. Houston, Tex.: Port of Houston Authority, 1989

Wood, Charles Raymond. *Milwaukee Road—West*. Seattle, Wash.: Superior Publishing Co., 1972

Yenne, Bill. *The History of the Burlington Northern*. New York: Bonanza Books, 1991

PERIODICALS

"The Alaska Railroad, Historical Summary," Alaska Rail Marine Services

Brouwer, Norman. "The Port of New York—A History: 1860-1985" (3 parts). *Seaport*, spring, summer, winter 1986

The Detroit Marine Historian, various issues

Deverell, William F. "The Los Angeles 'Free Harbor Fight.'" *California History*, spring 1991

Downing, Robert W. "The SP&S, the GN and the NP." Great Northern Railway, March 1996

Kemble, John Haskell. "The Big Four at Sea: The History of the Occidental and Oriental Steamship Company." *Huntington Library Quarterly*, April 1940

Michigan History, November/December 1993

Port of Chicago Magazine, September 1966

The Port of Galveston Magazine, 1972

"Port in a Storm: An Historical Review of the Founding of the Port of Seattle" (pamphlet), September 1981

Portage, summer 1986

Railfan and Railroad, various issues

The Sea Chest: Journal of the Puget Sound Maritime Historical Society, various

Southern Pacific Railroad Bulletin, various

Teichmuller, John. "PRR Ches Bay Barge Service & LIRR Car Float Ops." *Keystone*, summer 1993

Transfer, Rail-Marine Information Group, various issues

PHOTO CREDITS

INDEX